WORKING COWBOY

Ray Holmes on Snipper at Diamond Cross cow camp, summer 1978.

WORKING COWBOY

Recollections of Ray Holmes

By Margot Liberty and Barry Head

Foreword by Richard Slatta

UNIVERSITY OF OKLAHOMA PRESS : Norman

All photographs are by Margot Liberty or from the Holmes Family Collection.

Book design by Bill Cason.

Library of Congress Cataloging-in-Publication Data

Liberty, Margot
Working cowboy : recollections of Ray Holmes / by Margot Liberty and Barry Head ; foreword by Richard Slatta.
p. cm.
Includes index.
ISBN 0–8061–2692–2 (cloth)
ISBN 0–8061–3503–4 (paper)
1. Holmes, Ray, 1911–1995. 2. Cowboys—West (U.S.)—Biography. 3. West (U.S.)—Social life and customs. 4. Ranch life—West (U.S.) I. Liberty, Margot. II. Head, Barry. III. Title.
F596.H683A3 1995
978.7'1032'092—dc20
[B] 94-29445
CIP

The paper in this book meets the guidelines for permanence and durability of the Committee on Production Guidelines for Book Longevity of the Council on Library Resources, Inc. ♾

2 3 4 5 6 7 8 9 10

CONTENTS

ILLUSTRATIONS

FOREWORD

By Richard Slatta

For more than a century, cowboy memoirs have given us great enjoyment and added to our knowledge of the past. Charlie Siringo (1855–1928) published the first cowboy autobiography, *A Texas Cow-boy,* in 1885. His memoir received a warm reception from the reading public, went through several printings, and spawned a host of imitators. Siringo went on to set much of his life to print. According to J. Frank Dobie, "no other cowboy ever talked about himself so much in print; few had so much to talk about."

Now, more than a century after Siringo's pioneering effort, Ray Holmes adds his fine contribution to the venerable genre of the cowboy memoir. His recollections come from "fifty years horseback riding and looking after cattle," mostly in Montana and Wyoming.

Holmes was born during a blizzard in November 1911 near Hulett, Wyoming, on the Belle Fourche River in the northeastern corner of the state. He shares with us the adventures and misadventures of his youth. As a baby, he was thrown with his mother from a runaway buggy. As a button, he suffered harsh stomach cramps from a heady mix of Christmas candy and rhubarb wine. He takes us back to Depression-era nights, family and friends gathered around a wet-battery radio to hear *Fibber McGee and Molly* and, on Saturday nights, old-time fiddlers.

You will share Ray's tough times during the Depression, laugh at bunkhouse pranks, and shiver in a chilling blizzard of April 1955. You will come to know, like, and admire Ray Holmes for his humor, honesty, self-reliance, and cool-headed common sense. For example, "Horses are like people," says Holmes. "What works on one won't work on another. Some you can slap around and get their attention, and others you've got to use kindness to get them to work for you."

Between Siringo and Holmes, lots of other real and would-be cowboys set their experiences, real and imagined, to print. William Roderick "Will" James (1892–1942) wrote and illustrated several books. His works include *Cow Country* (1927), the autobiographical *Lone Cowboy* (1930), *Cowboys North and South* (1931), and *Smoky* (1926), still a children's favorite. James took liberties with the truth, including the relocation of his birthplace from Quebec to Montana. His folksy western prose and real-life experiences as cowhand, rodeo rider, and stunt rider, however, give his writings a feeling of authenticity.

Sensationalized fiction has often nearly buried the reminiscences of real working cowboys. Beginning with Prentiss Ingraham's (1843–1904) *Buck Taylor, King of the Cowboys* (1887), pulp novels gained a huge, appreciative audience. Ned Buntline, Zane Grey, Max Brand, and countless others enthralled readers with tales of blazing gunfights and hard-riding heroes. Purveyors of pulp worried more about increasing sales and circulation than about raising the nation's literary standards. Historical accuracy often took a drubbing.

Fiction writers who jumped aboard the cowboy bandwagon produced many forgettable, thoroughly inaccurate volumes. J. Frank Dobie (1888–1964) pilloried several pseudo-memoirs in his *Guide to Life and Literature of the Southwest* (1942). Dobie dismissed *My Reminiscences as a Cowboy* (1930) by Frank Harris as "a blatant farrango of lies." The Texan deemed "equally worthless . . . the debilitated and puerile lying" of *The Autobiography of Frank Tarbeaux* (1930), as told to Donald H. Clark. The plain-speaking Dobie also found little of worth in the *Memoirs* of Bryant B. Brooks (1939), "printed to satisfy the senescent vanity of a property-worshiping, cliché-parroting reactionary."

Fortunately, authentic memoirs and reliable firsthand accounts continued to appear in the twentieth century. Andy Adams (1859–1935) left us a lively novelized account of a cattle drive, *The Log of a Cowboy* (1903). Like many others of the horseback literati, the Indiana-born Adams took some license with the literal truth. His descriptions, however, rang true and appealed to readers who demanded realism. Adams offered an unvarnished portrait of cowboy life that stood in welcome contrast to the silliness and romanticism of the pulps.

The "Roaring Twenties" brought rapid social changes, urbanization, and the proliferation of automobiles and other mechanical gadgets to the nation. As the country rushed into an uncertain future, many people longed for the simplicity of bygone frontier days. J. Marvin Hunter compiled hundreds of autobiographical sketches into two volumes, *The Trail Drivers of Texas.*

Iowa-born Emerson Hough (1857–1923) mixed Chisholm Trail fact and fiction in his immensely popular *North of 36.* The book appeared in 1923, the same year Hough died. He understood that many readers liked a little romance in a frontier setting, a formula he also used in *The Covered Wagon* (1922).

James Henry Cook's (1857–1942) *Fifty Years on the Old Frontier* also appeared in 1923. Cook gave readers a real taste of life in the south Texas brush country and on the cattle trails of the 1870s.[1]

Writers who might bamboozle drugstore cowboys from Manhattan could not fool a real old-time hand. Many cowboys could read and write, so cowboy writings got intense scrutiny from knowledgeable critics. Memoirs add important details and spice to our understanding of different historical periods. Two-time Pulitzer Prize winner Marquis James, for example, illuminates turn-of-the-century Oklahoma life in *The Cherokee Strip*.[2]

Some cowboys had a flair for writing, but many did not. Collaborators sometimes helped move a cowboy's memories from under his hat to the printed page. Lewis F. Crawford of the North Dakota Historical Society, for example, aided Ben Arnold in producing *Rekindling Camp Fires* (1926).

Perhaps the most famous collaboration in cowboy literature came during the late 1930s. Edward Charles "Teddy Blue" Abbott (1860–1939) tried for years to interest someone in his memories of range life. Part of the difficulty was his unwillingness to sensationalize by adding phony gunfights and other contrivances popular in the shoot-'em-up market.

Abbott, in his late seventies, had little publishing success until 1937, when he met a young New York writer named Helena Huntington Smith. They teamed up in a collaboration that worked wonderfully. In 1939 their coauthored book appeared, the memorable *We Pointed Them North*. The book "is all Teddy Blue," recalled

Smith modestly. "My part was to keep out of the way and not mess it up by being literary."[3]

How appropriate that forty years later Ms. Smith's daughter, Margot Liberty, should team up with another sure-enough cowboy, Ray Holmes. Their collaboration, too, has produced a fine volume. Liberty brings to the effort considerable skills as a writer, interviewer, and anthropologist. In 1967 she worked with John Stands in Timber to produce *Cheyenne Memories.* More recently she wrote the foreword to *Hell on Horses and Women,* Alice Mariott's volume of interviews with ranch women.[4]

Barry Head rounds out the team for this book. Head and Liberty worked together on an award-winning documentary film, *On the Cowboy Trail* (1981). The Holmes/Liberty/Head effort shows that the authentic cowboy memoir has lost none of its charm or power. Just as in the branding pen or at roundup time, able teamwork gets the job done. Liberty and Head have done a masterful job of organizing sixty hours of audiotapes (two thousand pages of transcriptions) into this innovative, compelling book.

Of course, without Ray Holmes's lifetime of hard work we would have no book. *Working Cowboy* is more than an entertaining, evocative memoir. It is really two books in one. Every other chapter recalls events from Holmes's life, beginning with his Wyoming childhood and going through his retirement from cowboying in the late 1970s. Alternate chapters are filled with down-to-earth advice about cowboying and ranch work. Seven helpful chapters cover "Some Talk About" Cowboys, Calves and Calving, Working with Cattle, Horses, Herd Management, Breaking Horses, and Gear.

You will learn a lot from Ray Holmes, and you may find yourself itching to argue with him about some of his views. Ray, for example, sees little merit in spurs, and he gives you several reasons why. "If you're out riding in the hills and your horse falls down, a spur can catch on the saddle or a back cinch." Holmes speaks from experience. Likewise, he has no use for cow dogs. "I'm my own dog, and I've got my own tricks."

Like many retired cowboys, Holmes has a sense of being the last of his breed. Daniel G. Moore (*Log of a Twentieth Century Cowboy*, 1965) felt the same way: "I find myself one of only a small remnant of the old boys I knew." Ike Blassingame (*Dakota Cowboy*, 1958) lamented that "many of those I knew and worked with on the old cattle ranges of the north have gone to the Happy Hunting Grounds."

Of course, neither cowboys nor cowboying is gone forever. True, much has changed. But if you compare Charlie Siringo's memoirs of a century ago, Teddy Blue's of fifty years ago, and those of Ray Holmes, you'll find the same grit and spirit that have always characterized cowboys. *Working Cowboy* makes an admirable contribution to the real history and memory of cowboying and ranch life. Saddle up and enjoy the ride down memory lane.

NOTES

1. *Fifty Years on the Old Frontier* is available from the University of Oklahoma Press (1980).

2. Published, with a new foreword by William W. Savage, Jr., by the University of Oklahoma Press (1993).

3. Available from the University of Oklahoma Press (1991).

4. Margot Liberty's books include *Cheyenne Memories* (1967, coauthored with John Stands in Timber), *American Indian Intellectuals* (1978), and *Anthropology on the Great Plains* (1980) as well as the foreword to Alice Marriott's *Hell on Horses and Women,* (University of Oklahoma Press, 1993). She has also written more than thirty journal articles and chapters in books.

PREFACE

I met Ray Holmes in the summer of 1974. I was staying on Ellen Cotton's Four Mile Ranch, near Decker, Montana, when I heard someone drive into the yard. Strangers—sometimes Cheyenne Indians—would come down the four miles from the county road from time to time, and as I was alone, I went out to see what was happening.

I found a very cowboy-looking person with his wife, driving a white pickup. They were borrowing a grain loader. They hadn't stopped in to tell me because they didn't know I was there.

So began a friendship that has gone on ever since.

Ray Holmes, who was Ellen Cotton's nearest neighbor on Four Mile Creek, worked for the Diamond Cross Ranch several miles away. Ellen consulted him on ranch matters all the time, and he would drive in to her establishment quite often. Usually, Ellen had kids from the East working there, young relatives and friends from around Boston, and Ray loved to visit with them. He would come rattling down the hill in his pickup, usually with a saddle strapped to the side and a horse aboard. Everybody stopped work to go talk to Ray. He could solve almost any problem on a ranch, and he looked not unlike John Wayne or the Marlboro Man. He knew he was "local color," and he enjoyed it.

Sometimes Ray would borrow one of Ellen's work force—usually a girl who had done some riding back East—and take her out to help him move cattle. At that time he was cattle foreman at the Diamond Cross and its only full-time cowboy. The Diamond Cross was sizeable even by Montana standards, with big, rough pastures west of the Tongue River valley. There was a lot of summer riding, which Ray usually did alone. But he knew how to use green help. It didn't matter how ignorant you were, or how well you rode. In a short time he had you functioning. He might tell you just to hold your horse in a certain place, or to follow the cattle up a particular gully or draw. With another rider, he didn't have to cover so much ground.

By the summers of 1977 and 1978 I became his regular helper—at first commuting from Ellen's and later living in a bunkhouse cabin next to Ray and Pauline. We would start before dawn; by starlight I could see little but the red tip of Ray's Bull Durham cigarette. By sunrise we were up in the high country that formed the divide between Tongue River and the Rosebud, another northward-flowing tributary of the Yellowstone. This was prime summer pasture for Diamond Cross cattle. Ray used to call it "as close to heaven as I ever expect to be."

The Birney area of the Tongue River valley is one of the few unspoiled places left in America where there is a sense of vast space. Up on the divides are parklike areas of grass, studded with ponderosa pine and juniper. On top you can look across southward to the blue heights of the Big Horn Mountains. The blond grass is interspersed with red and yellow shale outcroppings, wild flowers, and silvery blue sagebrush. With the sound of wind in the trees and songs of meadowlarks, it is one of the loveliest landscapes in the world.

Ray never worked on dude ranches or competed in rodeos. As a working cowboy, hired to care for range livestock, he belongs to a historic and highly specialized occupation whose ranks are thinning with the passage of time. Ray says his skills are obsolete—the proliferation of barbed-wire fences has everywhere diminished the need for full-time riders. Today most ranch families, aided by modern haymaking and irrigation machinery, do almost all their work, including riding, themselves. Ray says, "There ain't many of us old boys left." He is referring to those who still possess the breadth and depth of knowledge and skill that is evident in the following pages.

From the moment I saw him, I knew Ray was the real thing. He used the authentic language of working cowboys. Forty years earlier my mother, Helena Huntington Smith, had taken down in longhand the memories of "Teddy Blue" (Edward Charles Abbott), an oldtimer who first came up the Texas Trail in 1879. The first-person account of his life, which they wrote together, was called *We Pointed Them North: Recollections of a Cowpuncher.* It has remained in print since 1939, more than half a century.

I began making tape-recordings with Ray in 1976 when he was doing routine summer riding at the Diamond Cross cow camp. Ray, Pauline, and I would drive up-country twenty miles through ten or twelve closed gates, with pickup, four-horse trailer, horses, saddles, and groceries. At the cow camp, Pauline assumed command of the kitchen in the main bunkhouse with its coal range and propane refrigerator. Ray hauled drinking water from the pump, chopped firewood, and mowed a path to the outhouse. Often I rode with him in the morning, after which there was plenty of time for battery-powered taping in the afternoons or evenings. If anyone got a telephone call, by radio, the horn blew on the white pickup, which would usually terrify the horses, who hung around the front door. A person could get run over.

At that time, I was on the anthropology faculty of the University of Pittsburgh, where I had introduced a course on the culture of the American cowboy. In 1977, through the University's Center for Instructional Resources, we began a video project for class use that focused on Ray and his neighbors, Ellen Cotton and Anne and Bill McKinney. We then raised nearly $200,000 for a documentary film. After seven trips from Pittsburgh to Montana from 1977 through 1980, we had the footage that in 1981 became *On the Cowboy Trail,* one of the hour-long films in the *Odyssey* series on Public Television.

All the while I continued my own tape-recording project with Ray, which resulted eventually in sixty hours of recorded material. Barry Head, writer and artistic director for *The Cowboy Trail,* agreed to continue as my collaborator when the time came to edit the nearly two thousand pages of transcription into book form. Both transcription and editing went on haltingly for several years; as labors of love, those tasks had to yield to other demands. As this book goes to press in 1995, Barry and I can look back together upon more than fifteen years when it was never far from our thoughts.

Seventy years in the range country of Wyoming and Montana, from 1911 to 1981, are preserved here. Ray's keen eye and sharp memory recall the days before rural electrification and gasoline engines, as well as barbed wire, changed the ranching world. In spite of adapting to new times and methods, he remembers the old ways of doing things—the good, the bad, and the funny.

His account also gives perspective upon something else—the role of the cowboy in the American Dream. More than any other figures, cowboys have come to represent America to Americans as well as to the rest of the world. Somehow they stand for freedom and self-reliance, for individualism and independence. Nobody quite knows why, least of all the cowboys themselves. Whatever the reality, the cowboy, in the angle of his hat and the swing of his horse's stride, has laid a powerful hold upon us all. And it is a real man, behind the myths of now and then, who has spoken here. Modern ranchers will find some tricks of the trade they probably never thought of; and many old-timers will find themselves in his words.

MARGOT LIBERTY

Sheridan, Wyoming

A NOTE IN MEMORIAM

Ray Holmes died on November 9, 1995. His widow, Pauline, who appeared with him in *On the Cowboy Trail*, still lives in the house they moved to in town after they quit ranching in 1980. She and Shirley's family are glad his book is now appearing in paperback, and that he could enjoy book signings at the two Sheridan bookstores, which drew many of his friends, some of whom may not have read a book in quite a while.

For more than a century, the cowboy has been a uniquely American symbol, and his attire and mannerisms are well known. Western movies, novels, and dude-ranch vacations still sell as widely as ever, along with tickets to rodeos (which keep increasing in numbers). But the occupation behind the symbol is largely gone. Ranchers and their wives today tend to dislike the terms "cowboy" and "cowgirl." "Cowbelles" was in vogue for awhile in women's beef promotion groups, but last I heard it had become "cattlewomen."

The art and science of handling large livestock began in this hemisphere from transplanted Spanish roots, with the gathering of wild range cattle in the south and the big drives north to stock the northern grasslands after the Indian wars. The real cowboys, who worked with cattle virtually full-time, needed a lot of space in which to perfect their skills. This space rapidly disappeared with the advent of barbed wire, still the foremost plague of horses and cattle. Still, some big pasture ranches survive, like the Diamond Cross, which we pictured in *On the Cowboy Trail* (1981), a PBS film in the Odyssey series. And I found in my notes from early marriage an account of gathering horses (on horseback) on the north side of the Missouri River. The owner had said encouragingly, "They can't run very far, only two miles east over here, and four miles west." Whether this particular pasture has been subdivided with barbed wire yet, I don't know.

Ray Holmes was one of the few authentic survivors, or diehards, and he was often dubbed "The Marlboro Man" by those who had to work in the hayfields or irrigation ditches. Most of the ranch year is taken up now in putting up hay summers and feeding it out winters.

A veteran ranch foreman on the Padlock (one of the biggest) told us once, "It's the damnedest thing how the laziest uselessest kid will get lively around a corral full of cattle. Jumping and running and messing things up." The work underway was sorting "dries" out for market, and the kid kept bouncing them back into the herd (dries are cows without calves who are often sold on the slaughter market). "Or they slam gates and they use a whip too much."

Ray Holmes taught that it is very seldom necessary to ride at a gallop, no matter what they do in the movies. A veteran herd handler can spend much of his time at a walk, or holding still. Ray was obliged to do a lot of his work by himself, the other men being of course in the hayfield. And he enjoyed it, calling the work in these pages "as close to heaven as I ever expect to be."

If you belong to Ray's school of thinking, you never, never use a dog, especially when working with cows and calves. The dog gets a mother cow "on the fight" and she will turn back to protect her calf, who often gets lost in the shuffle and can lose his mother permanently, a process called "bumming" a calf. (Bumming means unintentionally separating a cow from her calf—the calf, who still depends on his mother's milk at this time, stays alive on a few bites of grass and a stolen sip from a strange cow now and then, but he will never make a decent market animal. Cows and calves are mutually exclusive and do not permit milk raids from outsiders. Assuming that our drive is taking place in the spring, he would normally be with Mom until weaning time in the fall.) The calf runs off bawling, but everybody is bawling about the dog and he can't recognize his mother's dulcet tones. About dogs and other innovations, Ray would say: "I'm from the old school."

Nonetheless, a lot of modern ranchers use dogs, which are good at getting animals out of brush patches. But Ray went after them on foot himself. He told me, "I'm my own dog," and in the case of one dry cow, "She didn't want to be in that brush [usually ash, wild plum, or chokecherry trees] with me. If the calf runs away from the herd, he is just scared, and he gets more scared if you chase him so he runs faster. That's one time you may have to gallop to get around him, if you can; but he often goes through a fence (and can't get back), and the gate may be miles away. He wants to come back to the herd and usually does if you leave him alone."

These "drives" from one pasture to another are just about the only remnants of the big trail drive, when ten or twelve cowboys handled a herd of two or three thousand. Nowadays ten or twelve riders may be with a little herd, counting the owner and his kids and guests who want to participate in this vestige of history. This causes the little herd of say, one hundred, to widen out at the back because they are being pushed too hard, and can cause more bumming. A herd should travel stretched out in a column several animals wide. This way the leaders lead, the drags drop to the rear, and everybody stays "mothered up" (each calf with its own mother and vice versa), a term I once wanted to use for a book about my family.

Many activities with horses and cattle have lost their appeal for me, since so often brutality and rough handling are common, and the slaughterhouses await—this is true of rodeo, horse shows, and racetracks. And there is not enough horseback work on a modern ranch to justify the months of riding that make a trained cow horse.

I was really lucky to share Ray's long rides, which nearly always began before dawn. The scenery was beautiful once the sun came up, and we would be well on our way to the high country where the herds graze during the summer. And watching Ray (and pestering him with picture taking) was like a little taste of old times.

A memory I especially treasure is the episode of the Recalcitrant Bull. A big Hereford, he was needed uphill, out of his resting place, with the cows. But he had forgotten about the cows and didn't want to go. Solitary bulls have sometimes been "whipped out" of a band of cattle by a stronger bull, but he was not showing any wounds or bellowing any challenges. A perfect time for whooping and hollering, one might think, on our part. But no. We sat there on our horses. We were between the bull and where he'd been grazing. The rocky trail twisted steeply uphill behind him.

Ray rolled and smoked a cigarette. We sat there. He stood there. Ray moved a few steps to block him when he tried to get past us. Ray rolled another smoke. My horse grabbed a mouthful of yellow sweet clover, Bull Durham tobacco now scenting the air along with clover and sagebrush and pine. It was a gorgeous morning.

Everybody stood their ground. Finally the bull flipped his tassel tail and marched up the hill (more like a mountain) all by himself. We followed him. So much for whooping and hollering that day. Ray might tell us, "You know what you want to do. The critter doesn't know what you want. You try to get him to want the same thing."

When working with one or two strays the action often gets faster. The quarry is often in the wrong pasture and needs to be put through a wire gate. The rider throws the gate open and now tries to influence the quarry to (1) see it and (2) go through it. After three or four passes the quarry generally sees the hole and goes through it, at which the cowboy in charge will often holler in celebration, "The child is born!"

Some other amusing phrases (I think these are called "argot" when derived from a particular trade) are the following:

- "I come a-ridin' in."
- "A day late and a dollar short."
- "Take a deep seat and a short rein."
- "He was rode hard and turned out wet."
- "Around the horns" may have come originally from sea lore, but is used hereabouts in reference to the Big Horn mountains.
- A bouncy horse "could have shaken Christ off the cross."
- "That horse had rollers in his nose" (a special kind of snorting in high-spirited animals).
- "A face that had wore out three bodies."
- And of one individual: "He don't need a wife. He's a woman himself."
- Or perhaps it had rained "like a cow pissing on a flat rock."
- And today, "The child is born!"

Wonderful turns of phrase, wonderful memories. Ray, we know you are in the highest heaven there is.

MARGOT LIBERTY

Sheridan, Wyoming
March 2002

WORKING COWBOY

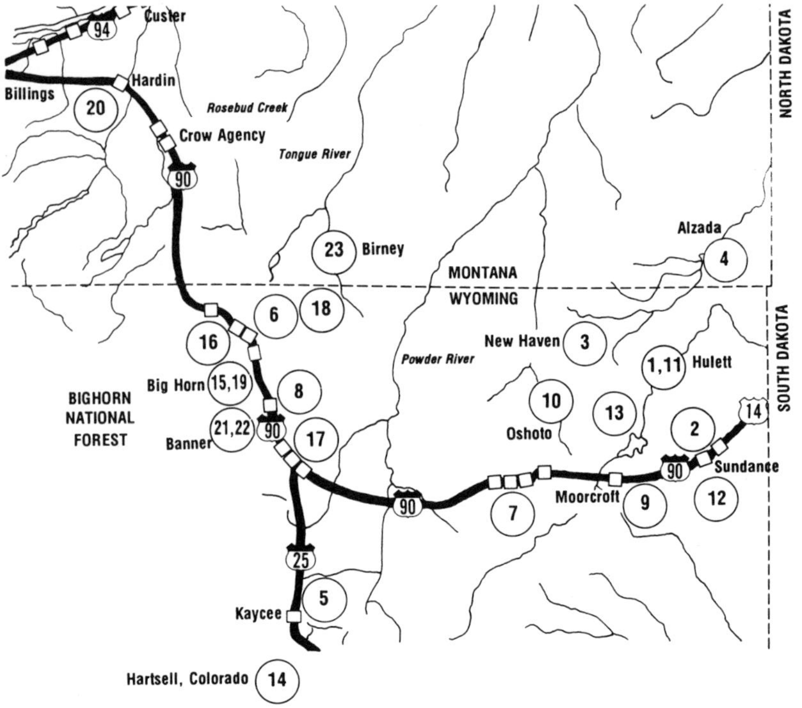

Ray Holmes Country

1. Hulett:
   Ray born, November 26, 1911
   School, 1919–1927
   Odd jobs, 1927–1938
2. Sundance with sister, 1932
3. New Haven, Winnie Richards Ranch, September 1934–September 1935
4. Alzada, construction job, May 1937
5. Kaycee, 3T Ranch, June 1937–September 1937
6. Sheridan:
   Pauline born, March 25, 1919
   Frybergers, June 1938–April 1940
   Shirley born, July 14, 1940
   Teunis Clark, Wolf Creek, August–November 1941
7. Gillette, Ray and Pauline married, January 1940
8. Sheridan, Meade Creek with Aunt Mabel Hublitz, sharecropping, April–October 1940
9. Moorcroft, McKean Ranch, November 1, 1940–mid-July 1941
10. Oshoto, D Ranch, March 1942–May 1942; LA Ranch, May 1942–Spring 1943
11. Ike Ranch, Spring 1943–September 1944
12. Sundance, Charles born, September 3, 1944
13. Devils Tower, Hereford Ranch, October 1944–April 1946
14. Hartsell, April–September 1946
15. Big Horn, Bar 13, September 1946–1952
16. Beckton, August 1952–June 1955
17. Buffalo, June–September 1955
18. NX Bar, Hamm Place, September/October 1955–April 1956
19. Hidden Valley, Spring 1956–Spring 1957
20. Little OW, Hardin, May 1957–March 1958; NX Bar, Calving heifers, March 1958 (six weeks)
21. Banner, Wagon Box Ranch (WBR), Earl Simpson, April 1958–September 1965
22. Duncan's, April 1966–June 1968
    NX Bar, October–April 1966
23. Birney, Diamond Cross, June 1968–November 1980

CHAPTER ONE

SOME TALK ABOUT COWBOYS

A cowboy has a carefree life in a lot of ways. You don't have to punch a clock. You put in long hours, and, of course, you can be out in all kinds of bad weather and think, well, by God, it'd be nice to be setting by the stove. The worst of it is probably in the winter time when you're short on feed, you're getting thin cows rustled out of the hills, it's cold, and there's no feed when you get there. When I was a young feller, there was a guy that used to say, "By God, if I had my life to lead all over again I'd set in a steam-heated office and push a pencil!"

But I like cows, and there's even times in the winter that are good—when you're scattering feed blocks, the cows are getting plenty of grass, there's only a little snow on the ground, and it's not too cold. Winter can be a joyful time, especially at Christmas when the frost gets on the trees, and the cows is doing good. It's a nice Christmas when there's not too much hard work to do and the days is short. That can be a really good time of year.

The best time of all to me, though, is in June when the grass is green, the cows are all scattered out, the calves are on the ground, and the branding is done. There's nothing nicer than to ride out on a good stout horse among a bunch of cows when they're all doing good, looking over the nice grass and knowing the cattle are all taken care of. I could do other work, I suppose, but I wouldn't put my heart into it. My pride and joy is taking care of livestock.

To be a cowboy, the first thing is to like to work cattle and horses. The two of them go together. You don't have to be riding top horses, but you need them in good condition. You can drive cows on a horse that's not so good if he's got a little cow sense. What I call cow sense is a horse that watches cattle, tries to learn, and is ready to turn a cow without you reining him in.

You have to be more or less of a horseman to be a cowboy. If you can work a horse, you can generally handle cattle, and if you have a pretty good kind of a horse, you can train him after cattle. Real cowboys know how to go out and ride a country, hold cattle up, work them, read brands, and sort them out the way they should be.

And you've got to be good working with men. You're not going to have all experienced men when you work cattle. You've got to be able to explain what you're doing, and if they will watch and go along with it, they can get by. When you go out on what's called "a circle" to round up cattle, they can help you put cows together and bring them in, even if they don't know much. So, that's one thing: to know how to string out a bunch of men and tell them what to do and where to be.

A man that knows how to handle cattle has his range figured out. He knows how to bring cattle out of the hills and where to bring them together. He will look out for other people's stock, be a good neighbor, get brands straight, and handle cattle nice and easy. There's a lot in knowing how to handle a bunch of cattle and what to do with them after they're worked.

Cowboys are not always good bronc riders, but they can do a little bit of everything on a horse to get by. Today bronc riding and the rodeo business is an athlete's job for arena cowboys. A young feller can go to these riding schools, and if he's a good athlete and learns to balance, he can ride a bucking horse. But when he gets done bucking, he don't know what to do with the horse.

These rodeo fellers never get a chance to work with cows. They only ride while a horse is bucking. When you get them out here in open country, they'll buck off as quick as some old farmer boy, because they don't know when the horse is going to buck. They don't have the feel of the horse.

And them contest ropers . . . when it comes to getting out and roping in the rough hills, they can't rope at all. They are used to making a charge on smooth ground on a good horse and the horse is working with them. On the outside, you are riding any kind of horse, running him over rough ground, and you have to bobble and dabble a calf. There's a lot of difference.

Most of the big ranches today are owned by eastern money or other wealthy people. I don't know right offhand of any that's owned by someone who started out from an early-day homestead. Most of the ranches have been sold and changed hands. There are very few native ranches. When I say native, I mean people that grew up on a ranch, people that's been right here all their lives. Right now I can't think of five people that has been around the ranching business all their lives and has places run now by their sons or such. If I really studied, maybe there'd be more, little places, maybe . . . dairies or something like that.

More than anything else, there is cowboys married to eastern gals who came in and bought them a ranch. The big end of them gals come to dude ranches, found themselves a husband, and set him up in business. It don't seem to happen so much the other way 'round. There was one wealthy eastern guy that married a hasher working in a cafe in Buffalo waiting tables, but that is the only one I can think of.

Some of them marriages worked and some didn't. The women had the money, and I guess if the husband went along, was a good manager, and stayed by his wife, why it worked. If he didn't, getting along would have been as hard as in any marriage. At a glance, I'd say more of them marriages worked than didn't. But anyway, there is a lot of eastern money scattered along the mountain up there that's been spent by eastern women.

Nowadays, ranchers have got to be farmers more than cowboys, and the farmers and cowmen are more or less friendly, because they have to work along together. In the early days, the farmer was plowing up the good grass that the cows would eat on, and they put in wire fences and cut the land all up in small pieces. But now, the cowmen goes with the farmers' daughters, like in that play *Oklahoma!*

You don't often see a good farmer that's a good cowboy. Some of them do a little of everything, but the one that knows how to farm is generally not a cowman. I can talk with people who do cow work a lot better than I can with mechanics and farmers, because we talk more or less the same language.

Of course, one of the differences between somebody who does this kind of work and somebody who farms, is that a farmer puts in his longest hours in the summer time. In the winter time, on a straight farming operation, he would be working on his machinery. He can kind of coast along during the winter time. He don't have to get out and hit the blizzards. When you're looking after cattle, the tougher the weather is the more you should be outside.

When the farmer's working hard along in July and August, well, if the year's good, and the cattle are more or less settled in the pasture, that's when I'm riding the gravy train. When you're riding horseback, you just can bicycle along, but the farmer has a lot of hard work to put in. His machinery breaks down, and he gets grease all over him. That grease is what I don't like. I don't mind cow manure, but I hate grease. Cow manure will dry up and blow off, but grease stays with you.

There's not really any old-time cowboys left. The men that went and slept out on the range and followed the cattle around . . . *they* was cowboys!

Of course, nowadays you don't have the hardships they used to. It's pretty modern, you ain't out very long, and you don't have to sleep in wet beds very often. Most of the cows is in pretty close, and you can do most of the work in a pickup. Riding is also cut way down with farming and machinery. Even with my job, I might drive clear to camp in the pickup, saddle up and be gone two hours ahorseback, and then come back. Or maybe pull the trailer way over there somewhere, get out and ride a little while, and get back in. So riding is cut way down, outside of just getting on a horse once in a while to go look at the cattle. The work with horses is getting scarcer and scarcer.

Cowboys are getting scarcer, too. Maybe there will be some guys thirty-five or forty years old come along, but there will not be many, and they won't get the experience that I did. I started when things was already getting tight. In the early 1900s it was big country, cattle were throwed out, and cowboys had to pull roundup wagons,

Unrolling barbed wire.

Attaching new brace support wire.

Tightening repair job with wire stretcher.

and do a lot of riding to get the cattle together. Then the country went to getting fenced up 'til, if the fences were good, the cattle stayed more or less on their home range. A lot less riding was needed.

Today, it's getting still tighter. More cattle are put in feed lots and smaller pastures so they can be looked at in a hurry. I don't ride near as much as I used to because modern outfits have horse trailers and stuff. You might cover a lot of country, but you don't actually ride as far.

I suppose a few cowboys will carry on down and do quite a lot of riding, but every year they're getting less and less. Young fellows can work for the coal companies, draw big wages, and make more money than they can ahorseback.

Knowing what I know about being cowboy, I'd have to say it's as poor pay as anything you could do. I would like to know why all these gals look up to a cowboy when, if they marry one, they're going to live on bread and water. That is what I can't explain: why people think it's such a glamorous life.

Everybody likes some things in life that others don't. I maybe could draw two thousand dollars a month at some other job, but if I had it all to do over, why I'd still rather get a-horseback and look at them cows.

I never made much money in my time, but I had a lot of fun.

CHAPTER TWO

MY FOLKS . . . AND WHERE I GREW UP (1911–1927)

I was born in November 1911 on my uncle Clyde Holmes's place ten miles from Hulett, Wyoming. It was an awful blizzard the day the old doctor come out with a team and sled to deliver me. I heard my dad tell about that a lot of times. It started snowing in October that year and kept a-snowing, and at Christmas time range horses was dying, because it had been a dry year and people wasn't used to putting up feed like they are now.

Women stayed home for childbirth then. The old country doctors went around over the country with a team and sled in the wintertime and with buggies in the summer. People never started going to the hospitals for childbirth until a little before World War II. After that, everything was in the hospital. But my sister, Lucy, was born at my uncle Cap Storm's place and my brother, Eugene, too. So my mother was never in a hospital for any of us.

The hospital in Belle Fourche, South Dakota, was fifty miles away. There weren't any cars then and it would be quite a deal to take someone fifty miles. I knew one boy whose mother was dead and who lived with his father and brothers, and the doctor told him he had appendicitis. So my mother and another woman went and cleaned up a room, the doctor brought a second doctor from Sundance, and they went up there and took his appendix out right at home. His dad and brothers looked after him . . . and he lived.

Old Doc Bostwick was the doctor I knew best. He was a county health doctor, and if he heard you had measles or chicken pox, he'd come out and stick a sign on your gate that you was quarantined. It used to be a $25 trip for him to come out ten miles.

Doc Bostwick was a big, bald-headed man who wore glasses, smoked a big cigar, and drank of lot of whiskey. Sometimes he'd come out so drunked up he didn't know what he was doing. If he liked you, he would try to get you well; and if he didn't, they used to say he might poison you just to get you out of the road. He'd sit around in Hulett and play cards most of the day. He had a little old office across from the pool hall and people would go get a finger taped up or whatever. He delivered babies all over the country.

My dad's folks came from Custer, South Dakota, in the Black Hills. My grandfather, Charles Anderson, was born in Sweden in 1850 and changed his name to Holmes when he came to America. His children were: my uncle, Clyde, born in 1882; my father, Mark Clarence, born in 1885; my aunt, Edna, born in 1889; and my uncle, Guy, who was an albino with snow-white hair, pink skin, and pink eyes like a rabbit, born in 1891.

Clyde went to Yellowstone Park in 1903 and run across Charlie McCoy, who lived in the Devils Tower country of Wyoming. Clyde went to look the country over and took a homestead there that fall. My dad came with him in 1904 with a covered wagon and some horses and took a homestead next to him. Guy took up land there, too.

My dad's homestead was right close to where my mother lived. I don't know how many years their courtship lasted, but they was married in 1910 and stayed on the homestead almost all their lives. My mother's folks came in from Colorado the spring of 1886. They were from Kansas and had stopped in Colorado Springs. They put up a cabin that year, and put a fireplace in it, but my mother's oldest sister was born that summer in a tent. They fenced up a little place to hold some horses, and they were there for the bad winter of 1886 to 1887 when a lot of people went out of business. It started snowing in October and didn't let up, and everything got iced down. I've heard my grandmother say them big Texas steers come in walking and bawling—and they died all along the river. That's the winter Charley Russell painted in *Waiting For A Chinook.*

My mother was born in a log house on her folks' place on the Belle Fourche River, and she never got more than three and a half miles away until Dad died in 1956 and she moved into Hulett. They went through a lot of hard times together on the old homestead. It's been vacant since 1957.

My mother was a small lady, and when I was a kid, she was the only person I ever saw riding sidesaddle. She used to claim it hurt her to ride a man's saddle, although in later years she did. She never worked cattle or anything, because we didn't have that many cows, but she'd get out and gallop right along.

She was a good mother, but she was very strict—a real old-type lady. She was a serious woman. She could have fun, but if anybody told a little dirty story or anything she'd get embarrassed. She didn't want us to get out with no wild parties or girls, and she always wanted to know where we was. A woman who smoked a cigarette or

Ray Holmes's maternal grandparents, James and Lucy Storm, with Sarah, Rosa, Nellie, Mel, and Jess.

drank any whiskey was down the drain in her book. She was shy of strangers and she didn't care to mix in big crowds, but she liked to have people come by, and she liked to cook up big meals. We always had a good meal set before us, a warm bed to sleep in, and our clothes was always washed up and clean.

My father could have a lot of fun. He was good to all of his family and a good provider. He was a hard worker with picks and shovels and teams. He was a powder man and shot a lot of rock. He wasn't what you'd call a horseman. He took good care of horses, but he didn't have much patience and he never cared about riding

Ray's parents, Sarah and Mark Holmes, 1952. *Courtesy of Mrs. Roger R. Rochford.*

broncs. He never followed the life of a cowboy like I did.

I must have throwed to my mother's side of the family. She had one brother, Jess Storm, that was horse crazy, and I've loved horses all my life. When I was a kid at home, I'd always be fooling with some colt. My dad thought I was wasting time and he would get provoked at me. He used to say he ought to put a barn right up beside the house, because I'd walk so far to catch a horse to ride a quarter of a mile. He'd ride a little on the small bunch of cattle we had—forty or fifty head—but he never cared to get out and go like I did.

He used to say I couldn't make a living on horseback. Well, he was wrong. I have done a lot of work in fields and with teams, but for thirty-five years horseback riding and looking after cattle has been the main thing in my time.

The house I was born in was built about 1910 before Dad was married. I came along in 1911. It had a rock foundation, and was built of logs placed straight up and down and sawed on two sides. Very few houses are made that way. It was stuccoed on the outside and plastered on the inside for warmth. In the wintertime, it took three wood stoves to heat it. There was no coal or modern conveniences. We had to pack wood in, pack water in, and then pack it back out again. You'd take a bath in an old washtub in the kitchen about once a week, heating the water on the old wood range, and taking turns like you would in a bathroom.

We raised one or two colts a year and that, more or less, kept us in work horses. My dad's horses started from two coach mares called May and June. They was fast, long-legged trotting mares, and hooked up to a light buggy they would really get out and drift. They wasn't broke very good. One time, when I was a baby, we was on the way down this steep hill to my grandmother's when they got scared and started to run. They run off the road, upset the buggy, throwed everybody out, and away they went into the trees.

My mother got throwed out with me in her arms and hit her head on a rock. The blood coming off her head put blood all over me and she thought I was dying. It was still a mile and a half to my grandmother's, but my mother was so scared that she took off down the road on a run. My dad tied up the team, and when he caught up to her, she was hysterical. He grabbed me, and I looked up and kind of grinned, so he told her, "Hell, he ain't

Ray Holmes, age two.

hurt!" And they got to my grandmother's and got the blood washed off and sure enough, I wasn't.

But the old buggy was tore all to pieces. It laid out in the brush and you can probably still see a spoke or two there today.

We generally had Christmas dinner at home. My mother would fix it, or my grandmother, and all the family was there. I remember one Christmas party, during moonshine times when liquor was against the law, and a neighbor brought over some rhubarb wine he'd made. I'd been eating a lot of candy and nuts. That was a treat, because you didn't get candy like you do today. And there sits this wine, so, when nobody's looking, I pours myself out a good shot and drinks it. It was pretty potent, and with all that candy and nuts, it give me such awful cramps I thought they was tearing me apart. I can remember like it was yesterday my mother heating china plates to put on my stomach. She figured out from the glass that I'd had some of that wine and she scolded me. I thought it was the best stuff I ever tasted.

So that was our Christmas, the family and neighbors getting together. We'd go out with a team and sled and cut a Christmas tree. We didn't get presents like kids do today—some candy in our sock, maybe an apple or an orange, and then old Santy Claus would leave a few nuts on the table. But I got a big top one Christmas—probably the best Christmas I can remember as a kid. I had tonsillitis, and I couldn't get out, and I spun that top all winter long. It had a winder with a spring, and that soon broke, but they showed me how to put a spool and a string on it, and I'd give her a jerk and that top would hum. I just set by the hour and spun that top.

Our homestead was 160 acres at first, then we leased some land and eventually got enough more to make 320. With my uncle, Clyde, in partnership, we were using 900 to 1,000 acres altogether. It didn't take the money to live that it does now. We'd sell some cream for cash, clothes didn't cost much, and nothing was fancy. There were no automobiles, and your house had no utilities—you used wood off the land and kerosene or gas lights. You produced most of your own food—your own meat and garden stuff that you canned for wintertime.

We used to milk twelve or fourteen cows, all by hand. My sister milked, and my brother even when he was small, and my dad and my mother. Any extra milk was fed to the pigs. A can of cream used to bring about five

Homestead dwelling near Hulett, Wyoming, where Ray grew up.

Garage and storage building at Hulett homestead.

dollars and we sold two of them a week. That was ten dollars coming in and that would more than buy what groceries you got out of the store.

The cream went to the creamery at Fremont, Nebraska. I would take a team and buggy and one or two cans at a time to the post office in Hulett, and they put stamps on it. It cost fifty cents to ship a five-gallon can to Nebraska, and the empty cans came back, so the mail carriers really had a job handling all the cream cans in the country. Many a time, I rode six or seven miles over to the post office and carried back an empty can on my saddle horse. My mother used to pack a cream can or a parcel-post package home sidesaddle on her gray mare.

There was a little dry-goods store in Hulett where you could get stuff, but most of our clothes came from the Montgomery Ward or Sears Roebuck catalogs. I have put in a lot of time on a saddle horse packing home mail-order clothing—overshoes and what have you. You grew up on a horse at that time and they didn't think nothing about sending a kid off somewhere to get something. It was be just like sending an automobile today. I remember one time my dad sent me twelve miles after fifty pounds of seed corn. They put it in a sack, laid it in front of the saddle divided on both sides of this old horse, and I rode back with the corn. I was twelve or thirteen years old.

Everybody baked their own bread. With six of us at home, we used to lay in half a ton of flour in the fall. We didn't grind our own. Dad would take wheat to the flour mill in Hulett, and they'd buy it, and we would buy our flour. Twenty fifty-pound sacks was a year's supply. We put them on wide boards hung up with wires in an old storehouse, so the mice couldn't get in.

We raised potatoes. God, I used to hate to bend over and pick up potatoes. We'd come home from school, and Dad would have them plowed out, and we'd have to pick them up and pack them into the cellar in sacks or buckets—whatever us kids could handle. Everybody had to pack potatoes. Or another time there might be 1,000 pounds of them in a wagon box set upgrade a little on a slope so the potatoes would roll back, and Dad would lift up the endgate a little and fill up whatever we could carry to the house.

Potatoes was a big diet. You had them damned near three times a day. We probably stored a ton and a half. We wouldn't use all of them, so when it got warm in May and June, you'd have to break all the sprouts off so they wouldn't spoil before the new potatoes were ready. We must have planted 400 pounds. Sometimes Dad sold them for a dollar a hundred. We used to put in big patches, because if they wasn't worth anything, you could feed them to the pigs. We would keep as many as four sows and raise between twenty and fifty pigs to sell, in addition to what we used for meat, and get a little cash out of the deal. It depended on how much grain we had around.

The sows were bred so they would have pigs about April, when the weather was warm. We might have a boar of our own or we might just take the sow to a neighbor who had one. To haul a sow, you use hog crates that you drop a little grain in to get the sow to go in, and then three or four men can set it in a wagon. One sow would have from five to eight pigs. The pigs suck the mother, and as soon as they are two weeks old, they can start drinking skim milk, too. Dad always raised corn and barley, so they was fed on grain and skim milk, and they ate the waste off the ranch. If a pig is fed good milk, in about six months he's a butcher hog. They grow that fast.

People don't know what work is today! There were butcherings at home when the neighbors used to get together and help one another, and my dad would kill six hogs in a day, and my mother would help him work all that meat up. You'd generally butcher once early in the fall—as soon as the weather cooled off so flies wouldn't bother the meat. If it was only one hog, you would maybe divide it up with a neighbor—each would take half in order to get some fresh pork. By then you were looking forward to it, because you had been eating cured pork all summer and were running out by then.

Generally, the big butchering was around Thanksgiving. You'd have so much meat and no meat house to work it up in, so you did it in the kitchen. You'd render all that lard, grind sausage and push it into muslin sacks the women sewed, hang it outside on the porch, and work up all the heads into head cheese . . . nothing was thrown away. You got so you didn't want any meat for a while, until you were rid of the smell of it. You'd be sick of it. I never did much cutting, but I had to grind lard.

A lot of pork was cured for the summer. You'd soak it for so long in a solution of salt brine, then take it out, wash it, boil the brine to keep it from getting sour, and then put the meat back in. After it got the right amount of cure, you hung it outside in the old meat house—a dirt-roofed shed that was cool in the summer.

Along in the spring, you built a hardwood smudge of oak or apple wood to smoke it. The fire was made to smoke. It didn't really burn. Boy, that was good meat! I've never et any today as good. When it was cured up, it would keep all summer long in a cool place.

Then you could dry-cure salt pork or bacon—put it down in a box and rub in lots of salt. My mother would slice some off and set it in a pan of warm water on the back of the stove. They kept it warm, changed the water a couple of times, and fried it when it had less salt so you could eat it. You sure couldn't eat it to start with!

It was a big job to get all that meat ready for summer. You could eat it fresh in the wintertime, but the rest had to be cured. We had other meat of course. Chickens would come to be fryers somewhere around the first of July. Then you'd eat chicken, sometime with some cured pork mixed in, until the fall. A lot of times my mother would kill chickens in the evening, keep them in cool water overnight, and we would have fried chicken for breakfast. So you'd get tired of chicken.

Then, somewhere along the line, you'd butcher a beef. If you could put it on ice, it would keep a week or so, but otherwise the weather had to be cold or you couldn't use it up before it spoiled. Most people butchered beef after

Thanksgiving when you could hang it up in some building. Of course, it was cut by hand, so if you wanted a chunk of meat in the wintertime, you'd go out and cut it off a frozen piece with a saw.

In spring, Mother would can a lot of that beef and we'd eat it quick. Beef couldn't be cured like pork. I don't know of any process even today that cures beef, unless it is corned or made into jerky.

There's no reason you couldn't keep on curing pork or game today if you had a place for it. We killed a deer one time, when a cousin of mine came to visit from Belle Fourche, and we smoked the hindquarters. This cousin's place is on Medicine Creek, and he called this meat Medicine Creek Bacon. We used it for breakfast meat and it was very good.

During an acorn year, you could have all kinds of meat. It happened every five or six years, maybe. I can remember two years in the '20s when there was a big acorn crop from the native scrub oak trees that are scattered through the Devils Tower country. The acorns start falling out of their shells in September or the first of October, and hogs will run and follow the trees and get real fat. They scoop them up so you can hear them cracking them like corn. Acorns are rich, but if you butcher a hog right off acorns, the meat is oily. It's not hard fat. But you can feed them some grain for thirty days to make the fat get solid.

You have to watch hogs in an acorn year, because they get going following the trees, and they can get away from you and in with somebody else's bunch and get sold. They don't come back home because they get all the feed they want elsewhere. And they are not marked like cattle. You can't brand pigs, because their hide is thin, and it would just make a bad scab and sore.

Turkeys eat acorns, too—sometimes so many they get them packed into their craw and it kills them. The craw is just under the skin and a turkey has to have rocks in his craw to grind up feed that goes into his gizzard. One time my mother had a gobbler whose craw got packed with big, heavy acorns he couldn't digest. So she put a slit in his craw, took out the acorns, sewed him up, turned him loose, and he lived.

So an acorn year was special, but every year there was lots of wild fruit. There were chokecherries, wild plums, buffalo berries or bullberries, a few wild raspberries and strawberries, and the folks had some wild grapes. And there used to be wild currants. They don't produce every year, but there was always plenty of fruit.

Bullberries turn red on the trees and make wonderful jam or jelly. Man, they were pretty and it don't take very many of them. My mother used to make buffalo butter out of them and it's really, really good. She rubbed them through a colander to get the meat of the berries with the little seeds all strained out. If they couldn't afford the sugar for jam right away, they canned big jars and jugs of juice and made the jam later.

One time we made chokecherry wine with some neighbors. We all went one Sunday and picked a fifty-gallon barrel of chokecherries. It wasn't fifty gallons after it was made, but it was good wine, and it would knock you for a loop all right. You put in the chokecherries and sugar and water and let it all ferment.

When I was a kid, the word cherries meant chokecherries. We hauled some hogs one time past a town called Alva—my brother and Dad and me—and Dad went into the store there and bought some canned cherries for the noon meal. I said I didn't want any, that I'd already ate a lot of cherries at home. But these were nice, big, red cherries with syrup on them. And I was an old green kid. All I knew was chokecherries, and, God, we had enough of them ourselves.

The folks would also get apples for the winter—some that would keep, and some cooking apples, and us old long and lank kids would eat apples at night with popcorn. My dad and another feller would take the team and wagon out to Spearfish, or Beulah seventy-five miles away. They'd put straw in the bottom of the wagon, pull into the orchards there and camp, and pick a wagonload of loose apples. They'd probably haul 1,000 pounds of apples each time, keep a bunch for themselves, and sell some to the neighbors by the bushel.

We made cottage cheese and butter for our own use and drank all the fresh milk we wanted. The calves was fed by hand on skim milk from buckets, after the cream was taken off for shipping to Fremont. The cream had to be kept in the cellar and, of course, it would get sour. They paid more for sweet cream, but it soured by the time it was shipped out. So that's the way we lived off the cows.

Refrigeration was an ice house. We'd cut big blocks of ice in the wintertime—fourteen inches wide and eighteen inches long, or different sizes—and store them in sawdust. Then, in the summer, you would put fifty pounds of ice at a time in a wood icebox that set in the kitchen. It was the only cooling we had. You didn't keep leftovers the way you do now.

Sometimes in the wintertime when there wasn't as much milk, my mother would churn the cream and make some good fresh butter and sell it at the store in Hulett. It was made in pound squares in a wooden butter mold—a square box with a handle on it. You'd smooth the butter in there and then push it back out and you'd have a pound of butter. You'd write your name directly on the butter, so if something was wrong, they'd know whose butter it was. Then you'd wrap it in butter paper and haul two or three pounds in a box to the store. Many a time I have taken butter to Hulett tied on behind my saddle.

On Sundays we made ice cream. We'd put a block of ice in a sack and beat it up real fine. Then we'd put it into the ice-cream freezer with salt. You'd turn it until it wouldn't turn anymore, then take the top off and clean off all the salt and ice pack, pull the dasher out, and then press it down and pack it. If you started by nine o'clock, by noon you could open it up and get your ice cream out. Then you'd have a big feed of ice cream and strawberries or raspberries, if you had them. The wild raspberries were slow picking, but they were really good.

The place was pretty much self-supporting. In good years, when we got rain, we raised corn, squash, tomatoes, beans, peas, and about everything else that goes into a garden. Also radishes, lettuce, and strawberries. Mother canned corn, beans, peas, and other stuff all summer. The cellar would be full. She had stuff left over that was never used in later years. She would make us kids go out and hoe the garden, and she had to do a lot of hollering to get us to do it. In later years, when our kids was little and Pauline had a big garden, I would hoe of an evening now and then, but I never did much garden work after I left home.

We were a pretty close family and we had a lot of fun living at home. My mother and father both believed in working hard and we all worked together. They always set a wonderful table of ranch grub. There was plenty to eat and a warm place to sleep. My mother made lots of them big old heavy quilts—carded the wool and sewed them together—and the house was cold, but nobody ever suffered from it.

We were lucky that way. We didn't have much illness. But, when people did get sick, they went to some doctor close to home and he'd give them pills. They never went anywhere else. And when a person died out in the country, they kept him right there at home, because there wasn't a morgue or anything. They would put formaldehyde on a cloth over his face, because a person's face turns black right away after death. Nowadays, they can pull blood out of the veins and make them look pretty natural, but in the olden days they couldn't do that.

When somebody passed away, they moved the stuff out of a cold room and put the body out on a table, or on boards laid on sawhorses. In hot weather, they put chunks of ice around the body until the funeral. They'd lay the body out straight, pull down the eyes while they were still warm, and put pennies or dimes on the lids to hold them shut.

Two neighbors generally came in and took turns sitting around the clock and changing the cloths on the face. The next day the body went in the grave, because that was as long as you could care for it. A lot of old-timers could help with a dead person that way, because it was the only way they had. I never did any of it, but my dad set with a lot of dead people. Nowadays, they take you to the morgue just as quick as they find you.

My uncle Guy Holmes, the albino, died at my dad's place in 1954, and his wish was that they care for him at home the old-time way. So they did that for him even then.

Back on those cold evenings when I was a little kid, we used to pop up a lot of popcorn. We raised some and would have it out in the barn. It got pretty dry, but you can put it in a snowbank for a while to take up some moisture, and then it pops like hell. We'd bring it in, shell a bunch of it off the cob, and maybe somebody would come along to play cards, or we played cards among ourselves. My uncle Clyde cut hair, and I've seen my mother get dinner for five or six extra people on some bad day when there was a storm, and the neighbors would drive in to get haircuts.

So we had a lot of good times. We went to dances together and rode many a mile in the cold. On long winter evenings, I thought it was great to get the chores done up, come in and set around, and eat popcorn and a big supper.

Another big attraction was the radio. We used to sit and listen hours to the radio like you do now with television. We had the first radio on the divide. Dad went into Aladdin after a load of freight one time when I was in the sixth grade, and he saw a battery radio working. He got excited and came back and ordered one parcel post—a Silvertone radio from Sears Roebuck. It took two big, dry-cell B batteries and one little C battery, or you could run it with a wet battery charged up like one for a car. He had to put up a wire aerial about a hundred feet long.

I come home from school one day and here was this music coming over the radio, and I thought that was the most wonderful thing there ever was. The radio was long and had a built-in speaker like a phonograph. So we had music in the house. There was no local news at that time, but you'd hear world news, and we'd set up and the neighbors would come driving in on Saturday nights to hear the old-time music. So it was a big thing. We hardly got any sleep that winter for a while.

Before spring, somebody else bought one, and then they came in everywhere. Clyde was always handy, and, to keep the batteries charged, he bought a little generator with a gasoline engine to run it. Other people had to send their batteries on the stage to Hulett, where it cost a dollar or so to have the batteries charged and sent back. Later, Clyde got a bigger generator that could charge five or six batteries at a time, so he used to charge batteries for the neighbors. He would let that old charging outfit run all day and part of the night.

Then we got two wet batteries, because we really liked the radio. We spent many an hour around it. You could run it three or four hours in the evening, but you couldn't get anything in the daytime. At night, they had plays you wanted to listen to. There was one called *Little Theater Off Times Square,* and we used to listen to *Amos and Andy* and *Fibber McGee and Molly.* Then, on Saturday nights, the old-fashioned fiddlers would come on 'til about midnight. Everyone used to look forward to Saturday nights. We didn't ever dance to the music—just listened.

The first train I ever saw was in Moorcroft, forty miles from home. My mother's sister, Rosie, was living there, and they were having a rodeo. So we hooked up the buggy and took along a camp outfit. A freight came snorting through where we were camping, and this old kid that was me about took to the tall timber. The horses heard the train beller on the crossing, and they pulled back, too, because they had not seen trains much either. We slept in tents and a train or two went through that night. God, with the rumble and blowing of those old coal-burning freights, we thought hell was right after us.

Cars came to the country about the time of the Armistice—about 1917 or 1918. One fellow came to our place with an old Overland. I suppose you'd have to go to a museum to see one now. It had a top over it with side curtains flapping along that you could use in the winter. Nothing was enclosed in glass. After Ford got to putting on glass in 1926 or 1927, people said they didn't want a car with all that glass. They thought that if you upset, the damn thing would cut you all to pieces.

I went to my first circus in my dad's great big touring car—an old Hupmobile. It was 1929, the year the crash came, and we drove in it to the Barnum & Bailey Circus in Gillette, seventy-five miles from home, out on a gumbo flat. There were elephants there, so it was a big circus, and because it was the last day, we got to watch them pulling it all down with work teams.

The Hupmobile was a good old car, but the folks got afraid to run it because they thought the tires had gone bad. Roads were rough, and tires would get down into the ruts which chewed up the sides. So the Hupmobile set in the shed for a year or two, until the folks traded it off for a team of horses, and then they got a different car that was a little better—a Chevy.

The guy that got the Hupmobile paid the back license on it, loaded it up with five or six kids, and drove it clear to San Francisco at twenty-five or thirty miles per hour. And when he got to California, he was still riding on Wyoming air.

CHAPTER THREE

SOME TALK ABOUT CALVES AND CALVING

We start calving in the spring around the 20th of March, because we generally put the bulls in with the cows about the cows about the 15th of June. It's a nine month period, just like with humans. There shouldn't be any calves after the 20th of May. The heaviest calving time will be around the 10th of April, for a week or two, and then they slack off. We'll take the early cows and feed them a little extra, and then I'll ride through the hills and see what I can see.

To identify cows with calving trouble, you keep on riding through them. If you're lucky, you'll find them. Last spring, I found a three year old heifer, that had never calved before, with a calf coming backwards. I drove her up to the barn and got it straightened out, but the calf was dead. There are a few like that. You can miss some, because there's no way you can see every cow in one day.

I would say an 80 percent calf crop is normal. Out of my own cows, there was 100 percent this year.

In a corral or in a shed, you generally throw down some straw and it's pretty clean. Out in the mud, it can get really dirty when you get blood and manure on yourself from the cow. When cows are full of feed and water it gets worse. Gant cattle don't have so much hay and stuff to come out of them.

I don't care to do much of it again. When I see people with a two year old heifer having trouble, I don't go up and volunteer to get the calf. I stand back because I know how much hard work and sweat you've got to put in. But, I can still do a few things that's pretty tough and still get a calf. A lot of people don't know how much pull you can put on a calf, or all the things that you can do to get him out.

Vets used to come out to the ranches, but very few of them will come to the country anymore. You've got to take livestock to the hospital. Everything is pickups and trucks and you haul the livestock right into town. The vet hospitals have cement floors pretty near like a person's hospital. And the vets make lots of money.

A three year old heifer has an easier time calving than a two year old because she is bigger. But even with three year olds, you don't get away from calving trouble. If it's the first time, any cow can have trouble. After they've calved once, they're pretty much on their own.

They figure you might as well breed them as yearlings and get their calves on the ground when they're two. Otherwise, two year old heifers get fat and don't breed as well. You'd think that waiting and breeding them at two would make for bigger cows, but vets tell me it's a proven fact that it's better to breed them as yearlings than to go to three because there's so many more come up barren.

Heifers calve easier when the calves are small. A person will feed his heifers one way one year and think he's really done something to make a difference 'cause the calves were small. But the next year, feeding the same way, the calves can be too big. Any time you got heifers, you don't want to keep them just on the feed ground. You want to let them graze, and feed them protein blocks as much as you can if the weather gets bad, so they get plenty of exercise. Fat heifers have a lot worse trouble calving than heifers that are in good condition.

At calving time, you should put two year old heifers in where you can watch them pretty close. You feed them in small lots where you can look at them several times a day, and at night you bring in what you think are the heaviest ones. Nowadays some people even have a night man that comes in to look after them.

After they have been calved once, you don't have to pay so much attention to them the next year. There is something about having one calf that makes it much easier the next time.

From the time a cow starts labor, it takes up to two hours to get the calf on the ground. Different signs let you know they're in labor. They're nervous and walking around, and they may lay down and get up a lot. After the water bag breaks, and nothing comes down after an hour or so, you check them. Sometimes they get the feet out, and they can go a little bit, but you can tell they're not going to have the calf. That's when you have to pull it.

When I have three or four heifers here myself, I look at them at nine o'clock, and if they are not showing any signs, all happy laying there chewing their cud, I let them go until about four. It's a pretty safe bet to do it that way when all you've got is a small bunch. But when you've got, say, a hundred or more out there, and you walk through them, it's easy for one to be just starting a little bit and you miss it. So you've got to check a large bunch more often.

A heifer needs time enough to dilate and start calving by herself, but you can also let them go too long. If you come by at midnight, say, and one's calving, my theory is to start getting the calf on the ground. Some people let them go longer, but I go right to work on them. Some cows is just slow, but when they don't calve after an hour or so of labor, there's usually a foot back, or the calf's coming backwards, or something else is wrong.

When a cow starts to have trouble, the calf could die by itself or the cow could kill it. If one front foot is back, the cow will push the head out, along with the other front foot, and then the calf won't move any further. The cow will keep on pushing and the calf will choke to death. I've pulled calves that had their tongues swelled clear out of their mouths and they still lived. It might take three or four hours for the tongue to get circulating and go back in the calf's mouth.

Calves can also die from just too long a time calving. They don't get out in time. And you can pull on a calf so hard that you unjoint his back. So many different things will kill a calf. Some even might have been dead when the cow started labor. Of course, they hadn't been dead too long because anytime a calf dies, the cow automatically aborts it.

Heifers can die, too, if they go too long calving or strain too much. Sometimes infection starts in. If a cow goes for a day with a dead calf in her, she stands a good chance to die. But sometimes they will surprise you and live.

I have taken calves out of cows in chunks. The cow couldn't have her calf, and it had died and rotted. You hook a hay hook into the calf's lower jaw and take it out a piece at a time. Talk about a dirty, filthy job! And there's all the fumes that come out of them. Then you fill the cow up with penicillin, and she'll be sick for quite a while; sometimes she will die and other times she'll live.

Usually, just as soon as you get hold of one of the calf's feet and start putting on a little pressure, the cow will lie down. Then you use a calving jack that goes right up against her rump. You put chains on the calf's feet, bring them back down to the jack, start jacking it up, pulling down towards the hind legs so the calf comes around in a circle and the head comes out. You call it "coming in a rainbow." That's the natural way. A straight pull is no good because calves are made to come around. Tightening the jack generally starts bringing the calf, and when you get the calves out past his shoulders, you really get the jack going fast, so the calf moves right on out without a hip lock.

A hip lock's what happens when the calf gets hung up at the hips. Its legs pull up in the pelvis and wedge there instead of sticking straight out. There are times you can pull on a hip lock and you can't break them loose, and then there are times when you can be standing there and the calf will just drop out by itself. The cow or the calf—I don't know which one—relaxes.

You find out a lot of things when you're calving two year old heifers. I've had it happen that a pull on the feet will flop the head back in the flank. Sometimes the head will come into the pelvis without the feet, or sometimes it's the other way around. I have used a haystring snare a lot of times. You tie it on the feet and push them back to the edge of the pelvis so the toes is straight, and then reach back with the string, and put it around the calf's neck, and pull the head into the pelvis. Rope is bad to put inside a cow to pull on because it burns or cuts them, and you can get infection. And a calf's teeth can cut your fingers when you reach in to get him. I've had my fingers gashed from them sharp teeth. Now they've got a shot you can give cows in the tail bone to keep them from straining. When they're not straining, you can push a calf back and around.

Sometimes a calf has one foot back. It happened right here in this corral one time—you could just see one foot and the nose. So I got the cow roped and shoved the head back, and God, it was hard to shove the head back and get that foot straightened up! I had an awful time keeping her from straining, getting that head back far enough to reach down and straighten the foot out. As soon as the foot was straight, she might have had the calf by herself, but I went ahead and pulled it out. It pulled easy.

But I've also killed heifers pulling too hard on them—and still didn't get the calf. It's easier to set and tell about pulling calves than it is to do it.

Before cesarean operations came in, if a calf was too big you'd have to put a chain on one foot and pull it out. You'd cut around the ankle and split the hide from the brisket down the front leg. You'd use a crooked knife with a ring on it. A calf's muscles are not tight, so you can work the hide back until you get it over the knee, and keep working with a calving jack. Pretty soon the shoulder pops right out of the hide. That gives you enough room so that you can throw a chain around the head and pull it out.

I've worked like that on calves that hip lock. You have to cut the calf in two, push him back, turn him around, and take a hind leg off. Of course, the calf is most generally dead before you start chopping him up. After a little practice and seeing vets take them, I got so I could cut them out myself. A lot of people used to do that, but nowadays you haul them in to the vet's, and they cut open the flank and just reach down in the calf sack and take them out.

Then there's the prolapsed cow. That's when her insides come out before she calves. You can sew the insides back in, but you should mark those cows, or keep them in your mind, and sell them in the fall if they get healed up, because it will happen again. I sewed up one cow, and even so the calf came right out under the strings, broke the strings, and was on the ground the next morning! But you should cut the strings, or the calf can hang up and die. You should never keep a heifer calf from a prolapsed cow. It's hereditary and carries down through the line like cancer eyes and other problems.

Something the vets do now that eliminates a lot of calving trouble is to pregnancy test heifers in the fall. They can tell the ones with a small or twisted pelvis, and they're the ones to put in the shipping bunch and sell and let somebody else worry about.

When the calf hits the ground, you pick him up in the air, give him a hard shake, get his mouth cleaned out, pound on him a little bit, and work his heart. Some people have a spike or hook of some kind, and they keep chains right handy to put on the calf's hind feet, so they can just hang him upside down for a while. When a calf comes backward, he can drown awful quick. When you hang them up, a lot of stuff drains out of his lungs and runs out of his mouth, and that drains it out of their lungs, and you can bring him around.

A hip-lock calf dies very quickly because the navel cord breaks, and whenever you break the navel cord, a calf has to start breathing on his own. I had one here this spring that I thought was dead for a little bit, but we just kept pumping his heart and shaking him, and pretty soon he started breathing and come right out of it.

Roping cow with prolapsed uterus.

Helper on other end of rope.

Roper holds cow snubbed to tree during surgery.

When a calf goes wobbling out, and he can't walk very good, you kind of push him and he'll wobble along, and you can get him out to where you have some straw, and he will lay on it until he gets a-going.

If a cow has a calf in the daytime, and if the cow's got good teats, and the calf gets right up and sucks, you can push them in with your other cows and calves. The same goes for calves born in a shed overnight; if they are up and sucking, and the weather's not too bad, you just wobble them out the next morning and put them over with the others.

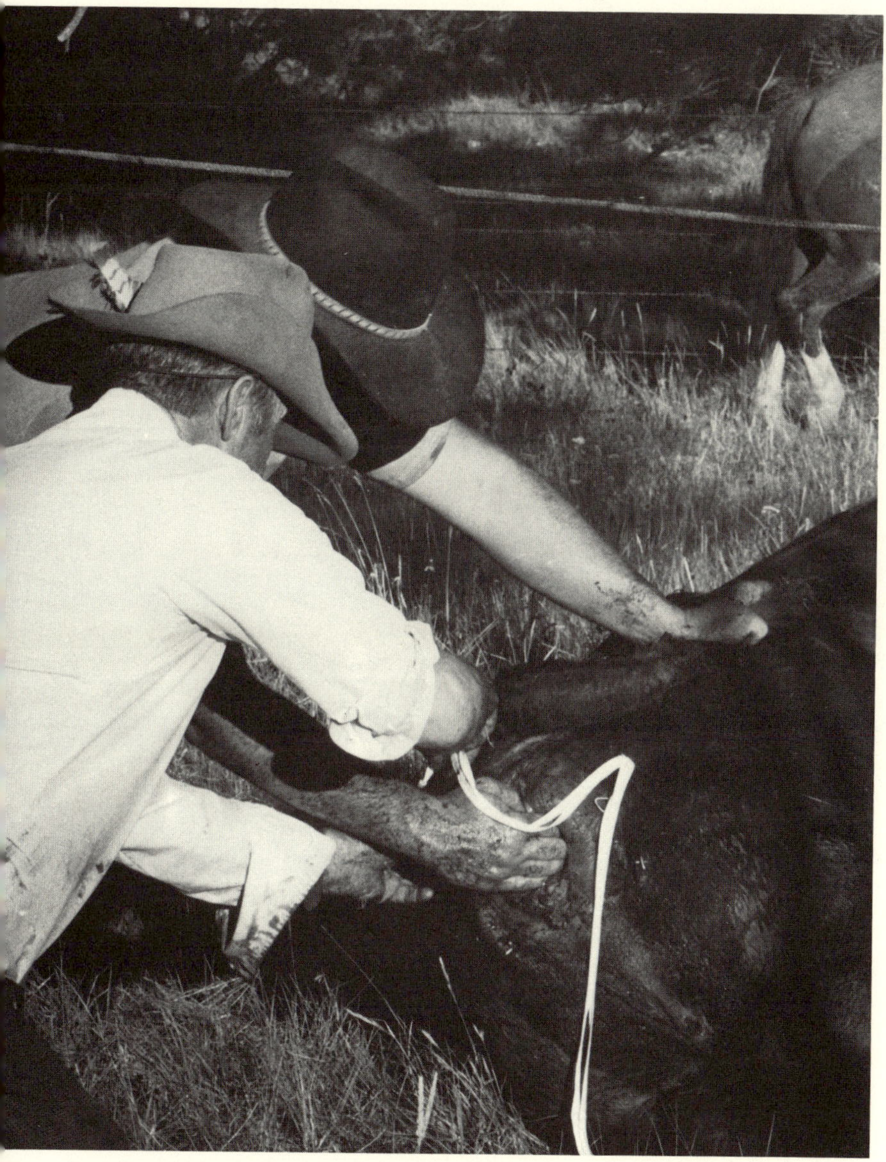

Uterus being pushed back into cow.

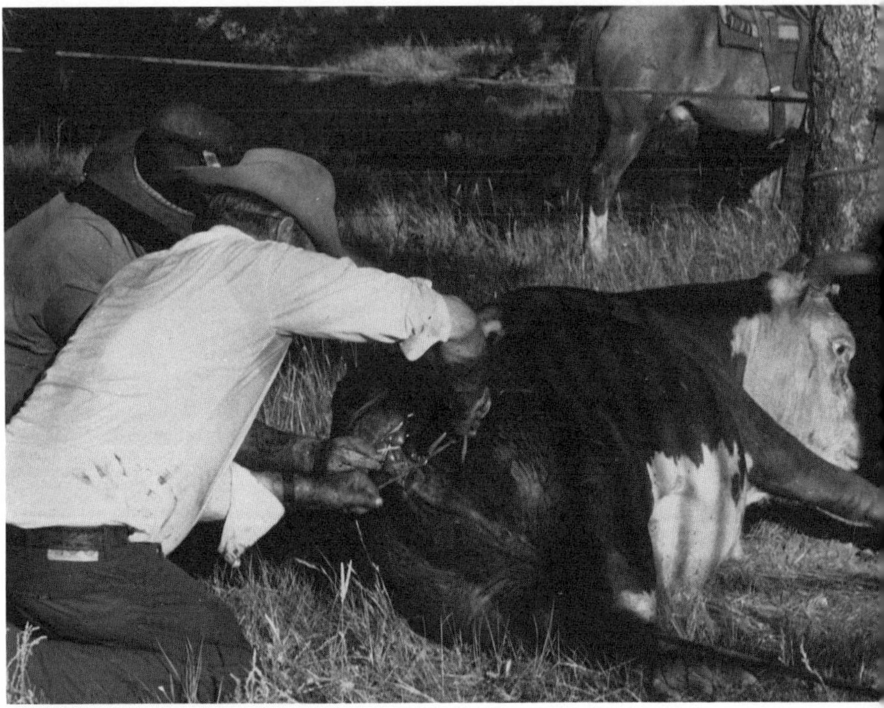

Uterus being sewn into place.

In the late Seventies, we had nine below zero weather in April and everybody lost calves. Between Billings and a seventy or eighty mile radius, they said 5,000 head of calves were lost due to cold weather, and scours, and spring sickness that got into them. It was the worst I ever saw.

Everyone was packing in calves, trying to keep them alive. You can get out here at night in the hills, and a calf is born at about dark, and by the next morning, if you do find him, he is dead. The cows hunt shelter wherever they can. When it's nice weather, the calves can more or

Cleanup following repair.

less go along, they can live. I've found them twenty-four hours old that hadn't sucked, but the weather was warm, and if you can get some milk into them and get them started, they are okay.

But on those awful subzero days, the cows' teats get frost on the end, and the hide gets tough, and it takes warm weather to peel the ends off. A lot of cows would drop a calf, and if you wasn't there to get her teats broken open, the calf couldn't get no milk and he'd die. On a range operation, you can't get to all them calving cows, and there's a lot of calves that can't get up in subzero

Some welcome refreshment.

weather. If a calf can't get something to eat as quick as he gets on his feet, it don't take long 'til he chills down and dies.

Cattle here have an advantage because it's rocky and gravelly ground, and with a little sunshine, it dries off. The ground is covered with pine needles, and it's almost like being in a shed. In other countries, deep gumbo can cause calving problems. When mud gets deep, like it does up on the Crow Reservation, there's a lot of calves lost. I think it was that bad spring after it begin to break up, when the mud got so deep that the cows would drop their calves, and they'd be muddied and couldn't get up. I've lost a lot of calves from mud. But this is a wonderful calving country if you have the feed on the range.

When you move cows where you can't count your pairs, and know that every pair is mothered up, a cow and a calf might end up two miles apart. You always take and turn the cow to where she can get back, and she'll trot right back to where that calf sucked the last time. The calf will wait there, too. He'll wait there 'til he gets starved out or gets bummed—meaning that he gives up on his mother coming back, and weans himself. After about three days both the cow and the calf forget about each other, and then you've got what you call a "bum" calf. The calf is weaned before he is ready, and he never gets enough to eat to grow out properly. They call them "potty" or "poddy" calves, too, and I've heard them called "beaver tails" as well.

The cows will look for their calves among the bunch and start picking them up. As soon as her calf sucks, that old cow's contented, and the calf follows her off, or lays down. You can always tell the cows that haven't got a calf because they're walking around bawling. The cow will be bawling with a tight bag and really tell you that she hasn't got a calf. Sometimes it's hard to tell 'til a cow's bag tightens up with milk, but then she'll start running and looking for her calf.

A calf can get bummed when you're moving cattle, and you can bum a calf even in a big branding where they brand a lot of calves. Cows can get tangled off, and the calf gets wandering off and loses his smell wandering among the bunch. Every calf has got his scent on him, and a cow can smell that calf.

Trucking is bad for bumming calves. You can know that a calf belongs to some cow, but if she's been down in the mud in the truck, and he's gotten manure over him and rubbed against other calves, the old cow just can't figure out it's her calf. A cow's generally got to smell a calf a time or two after they've been trucked before she really recognizes her calf.

If they're older, potty calves sometimes will take a little milk off other cows. When a cow is suckling her own calf, the bum will slip up and suck from behind before the cow realizes another calf is sucking. They can go all summer just nipping on grass if it's fairly good grass, and I have seen some bums that was pretty good looking calves. But generally after they get a little older in the fall, they'll be poor, hard looking calves.

If a cow is in a stanchion, you don't have to do much to get a strange calf started. Cows in stanchions are used to coming in and are used to calves sucking, and they don't see what calf is on them. But a calf has to get a little hungry to suck a strange mother.

The way we used to do that—if a cow was halfway gentle—was to have the calf tied up halterbroke and let him suck his own mother beside the strange cow. When he's missed a feed or two, you'd let him get a taste of the strange milk. Then you'd throw the rope under the cow and jerk the calf right over to the nurse cow, and here's a teat in front of him and he'd go to sucking. The cows were used to changing calves because when one got big you'd put on another.

If a calf dies, you can skin him out, throw the hide over the new calf, tie it around his front shoulders and under the belly, and let the tail hang over the back end. A cow will always turn around and smell the back end of a calf, so you want most of the hide on the back end. I've put big calves on cows with just a little bit of hide, but if that smell gets onto the back end, they will let the calf suck—and then turn around, smell the head and butt them over. They could tell the front end was wrong because the head wasn't covered up.

A cow is always smelling of a calf, but I never saw a calf smell of a cow. But a calf knows his mother's bawl. They know the bawl of each other. You can hear an old calf go walking out here and bawling, and an old cow'll look up and bawl, and then the calf will just take off on a high gallop. They recognize the voice, so they are pretty smart.

Angus cows will fight for their calves. They are good mothers. I once roped this calf afoot and pulled him up to a tree so I could snap a tag in his ear. The old mother cow bawled and came after me, and I could see she was going to hit me. Then another cow heard the calf bawling and she came after me, too. It wasn't a very big tree, and it had limbs right close. I had to drop the calf and crawl up the tree. You can't beat two cows around a tree, and cows will hit you if they get mad enough. If you have nerve enough to stand still, maybe not—but my feet won't stand still that long.

After calving, the next big event in a calf's life is the branding operation in May or June. Branding is the only way you can keep your cattle straight in a country like this. You've got to have a brand on cattle, because if everybody ran slick—unbranded—cattle, nobody would know who owned what.

They say there was a guy who had the "Maverick" brand and who wasn't going to brand his cattle. He just turned them out. If I remember right, he was a lawyer, and got a few cattle, and turned them out slick. That was going to be his brand—no brand at all. But soon he didn't have any cattle left, because everybody came back from the Civil War and went to branding cattle. That's how slick cattle came to be called Mavericks.

You could put tattoos on cows to identify them, but they would all have to be run into a chute to be identified. A brand and an earmark that corresponds with the brand gives a pretty good identification for a cow from a fair distance. If you don't see the brand, you see the earmark, although some earmarks may freeze out. And in the winter you can't read brands too well, because of the long winter coats the cattle grow. A lot of people have wintered cattle they thought was theirs, and in the spring the cows shed off and the people found out they belonged to a neighbor.

An ideal branding crew is one roper and usually three sets of wrasslers—two men to a calf. Then you have a brander, a vaccinator, and a knife man who earmarks and does the castrating, and somebody to dehorn. You have to keep a tally on them, and they generally have some woman or boy doing that. They look at the calf that's on the ground and mark it steer or heifer. You put a mark down for each calf and run a bar through them for the fifth calf.

The only other way I knew how to tally 'til I come here was to keep all the ears from the heifers, and keep the end of the bags from the bulls, so when you got done you counted all the ears, and then counted all the bags to find out how many bulls you'd made into steers. Nowadays there's too many dogs around. They'd eat up your tally before you got done.

Branding is kind of a neighborly affair where everybody helps each others. It can be a party time, too, but to my way of thinking, beer is fine after branding—after it's all over, with a good lunch. You get a little beered up while you're branding, and you can mess up with the vaccinating, the castrating or the dehorning, and you got to remember, it takes a year to get a calf on the ground. Besides, when somebody gets beered up, they can cause a wreck around the cattle—roping or wrassling. Somebody can get hurt, too—cut, burned, or jabbed with a needle.

When you're branding, you castrate the bull calves to make them into beef steers. There are several different ways to castrate. With small calves, some people cut the end of the bag off and pull the cords out. There's two cords—the blood cord and another one. They pull the blood cord down 'til it breaks off kind of jagged and closes itself. Some people take a pointed knife and split the end of the bag, and then split the cords. Another way to castrate is to cut a slit on each side of the bag, take a testicle out each side, and then scrape both cords off. The trouble with a slit on each side is that they can swell and plug up so there's no drainage. I have also seen where they bled pretty bad when the end of the bag was cut off. If hard blood gets packed up in there, they start swelling because the infection can't get out. Then you have to catch them, and take the clots out, and split the bag four ways to make a drainage hole.

Another way to castrate calves is with rubber bands. The bands squeeze in real tight, and the cords go dead. Then it grows over with new flesh, and the dead flesh drops off as the rubber bands keep cutting in. It takes about three weeks for the rubber bands to work. It probaly hurts worse than a knife until it goes dead and numb in there. I used them on my calves, and after an hour and a half of getting up and laying down, I guess it went numb, and they was traveling real good. That's a good way to castrate bigger calves, with bigger testicles, that could die if you cut them with a knife. There's no blood and no infection.

It's around feed lots and corrals that calves get infected from getting manure in the knife cuts. That's the worst poison there is, that manure poison, and it's all around barns. I've castrated a lot of big yearling bulls with rubber bands, and I never lost a one. So rubber bands are fine around manure and infection, but when you're out on clean ground, why I still like a knife better.

Sometimes, but not very often, you find a calf dead after branding, and you wonder what killed him. There can be freak accidents of course, but dehorning, castrating, branding, and vaccinating puts a lot of wear and tear on a calf. They can just die of shock.

CHAPTER FOUR

HORSES AND SCHOOL DAYS (1918–1927)

Horses were important to me from the time I was very small, and I have owned and forgot a lot of horses. My first horse was given to me by my dad, just when I was learning to ride. He was a bay horse, stocking-legged behind as I remember, and a star on his head, and I thought I had the world by the tail. He had a 76 on the left jaw, just like a 2 upside down. My uncle, Jess Storm, broke him to ride during the summer and turned him out in the fall.

It was a really nice November that year, and we had a dance around Thanksgiving at the big house that was my Uncle Clyde's first homestead. The old house had a pretty good floor in it, so they'd have dances there. It was a moonlight night, and some of the people coming to the dance met quite a bunch of horses moving out on what they called the Wilkie Place Divide. Nothing was thought about it at first, but then people began to miss their horses. It turned out that night some horse thieves took a lot of horses that different neighbors had turned out and my little bay horse was in the bunch.

We looked for the horse, and they never did hear of him for a long time. Then, my Uncle Jess was in Belle Fourche shipping cattle, and he saw a guy riding this bay horse. He knew the horse right off, even though he'd been gone for a couple of years. So he went over and asked, "Where'd you get that horse? I'm sure I broke him to ride." The horse had an 18 on his jaw by then—a worked brand. They had put a bar through the upside down 2 and put a 1 in front of it. And the guy said, "Well, you probably did. I bought him off Bob McNeilly."

This Bob McNeilly was a noted horse thief. But there was no way to get the horse back. He had been taken from Wyoming, and had the brand worked, and by then the guy owned him in South Dakota, and there was nothing you could do about it. People weren't strict about bills of sale then like they are now. You could buy a horse and never get a bill of sale, or you could get a phony bill of sale. And a guy that studies it can fix one brand into other brands all right. I've seen fellers setting around the bunkhouse for a pastime, figuring out what you can make out of a brand so it'll look kind of neat, but read altogether different.

Anyway, this McNeilly had a pretty good-sized ranch, part in Wyoming and part in Montana, and it was quite a while before people knew what was really going on. But one slick horse—a woman's pet horse that she could prove and everything—finally sent McNeilly to the penitentiary, and he died a broke man.

My dad gave me that horse about the time of the Armistice, I believe, so I would have been about seven. We never had electricity or running water, but the old phone line was in as early as I can remember. It was a country line running forty or fifty miles that people built and took care of themselves. It went into Hulett, so you could talk long distance. There was a lot of neighbors on one phone—maybe ten people on the same party line—and every time somebody picked up the receiver, it would weaken some more. Everybody had a ring—so many longs and shorts—and you'd grind her out yourself. If you called long distance, you had to call the operator. That was one long ring the same as "O" is now.

One time a neighbor's son got appendicitis, and so many people picked up the phone he couldn't hear the doctor. He hollered at them to hang up and he would call back later with the news. He said, "Christ, they was rubbering all the way to Rocky Point."

They had dry-cell batteries eight to ten inches long, as big around as my arm, and every year you would have to put in some new ones. They didn't use telephone poles. Everybody bought so much wire and kept up their own line. In later years, they kind of formed a corporation, and then a fellow by the name of Cook took it over, but you still had to do your own work. When they eventually put in modern telephones, my dad bought all that old telephone wire and rolled it up from Hulett. He used it on another community line up toward the Missouri Buttes.

In 1918, my dad freighted wheat thirty-five or forty miles into Moorcroft. It would take two days going in loaded and one day coming back empty, leaving Moorcroft early to drive back home. My grandmother would see him go by and call on the telephone, and us kids would go out to meet him.

He hauled wheat all that winter—fifty bushels to a load. Wheat weighs about fifty pounds to the bushel, so that would be 2,500 pounds—almost a ton and a half for the team. Nowadays they put 20,000 pounds on a big truck. That's as much as they haul on railroad cars. I wasn't even going to school at that time, but I can remember going out to meet him when we'd hear he was coming in.

That same year we heard the news about the Armistice. They would call the news out on the old telephone because it was before the radio. They would ring the one long ring for Central, and people would get on, and the telephone operator would tell if we was getting pushed back, or what ships had been bombed, or whatever. I never got to listen because my dad did that. But he was up at the barn when the news came that the Armistice was signed, and my mother hollered at me to run up and tell him that we had peace. I hardly knew what was going on, but I ran to the barn and told him the war was over.

So, anyway, that year of the Armistice was the year the first horse I owned was stolen, and I never got to ride him a day. I learned to ride on something else. Dad didn't have very many saddle horses, because he was a farmer. He had some work horses that he used to ride and work, both. One was a big, old, gentle work horse called Ben. He weighed 1,600 pounds and had been ridden when he was younger, so you could get him around a little. I'd get a bridle on him and crawl up a fence to get on him bareback. I'd ride aways, and then he wouldn't want to go where I did, and I'd have to slide off and lead him aways. He wasn't really balky, but he knew I couldn't control him. So I first started riding bareback on Ben.

Another horse I owned was Ribbon, a black, bald-faced, cold-blooded mare that was given to me by my uncle Guy the year I graduated from eighth grade. I thought she had died in the April blizzard, because she was an April colt sucking her mother then, but she came out of it, and I went ahead and broke her to ride and used her for many years. There was Red and one called Brownie that I broke and rode for quite a while. There was a little sorrel mare, Fannie, that we used to ride bareback, and a gray mare named Kit that ran me all the way home from school one day. Her little colt had just been weaned off her and was locked up in the corral. When I got on her at school, the gates was open and she went home in a high lope, nickering for that colt. I couldn't hold her. I couldn't do nothing but ride as fast as she was going. I went home a-sailing, scared, and came in bawling, "The old mare run off with me!" So I didn't ride her any more until we got the colt weaned off.

Ray with Whitey, Lucy, Eugene, and Mark. The pony's legs straightened up somewhat after he saved Ray from the rockslide.

And there was Whitey, the Indian pony that belonged to my sister and was gentle as a pet. At first, I rode him bareback, and later, I fixed a pad that went around him, and I tied a coat in front of me so I wouldn't slide off quite so easy. Then I got two stirrups on a leather strap that I'd throw over him. I'd get on a fence or higher ground to get on and put my feet in the stirrups. As long as you kept balanced on the horse, you was all right, but that pony used to shy, so me and the stirrups would hit the ground. That stirrup arrangement gave me a lot of balance, and I rode many a mile that way. Like they say, you need to keep a leg on each side and your mind in the middle.

That Whitey probably saved my life one time when I was in the seventh grade. My dad sent me to look for some cows down a winding trail that went into a high, narrow canyon. There were big overhanging rocks there and it had been a wet spring. I go riding around this bend and suddenly the pony wouldn't go no further. He whirled around and came back at a run, and then there was this awful crash and boom. We fairly sailed out on top of the canyon. When my dad and I looked down later on, we saw tons and tons of rock and dirt that had slid down. Some were rocks as big as a room that had crashed to the bottom of the canyon, slashing off pine trees as big as six inches across. Whitey must have felt the tremble in the ground. They say animals can sense a thing like that.

Later that spring, a kid from school, called Stanton, and I chiseled out a horse on one of the big flat pieces of fresh fallen rock. It was a big horse, twice life size. The rock laid really flat, and we could look across from the house when the sun was shining just right and see it. As years went on, the rain and wet weather made that mark get bigger. It kind of widened itself out with the wind blowing on it. It was there for years, until they put a uranium road in and pushed it upside down with a cat. We had cut our names on it and thought it would be a permanent landmark, but time changes a lot of things. Someday someone will turn it over and wonder what the names are that's represented there.

I always liked to do anything with horses, even though there was nothing outstanding about the ones we had. They was just work teams and saddle horses, not even good cow horses, because we never had enough cattle for them to learn much. I started plowing when I was ten or eleven. We put three gentle old horses on a riding plow—a sulky plow—one wet August, and I was so eager to get out and plow that my dad used to come and stop me. I wanted to put in more hours than the horses could stand. I always wanted to be a man before I should have been, working with him or doing something by myself. I'd get some wood or hay with a team, or clean out the barn, or ride off to the neighbors, and think I was doing a man's job. Lucy and Eugene always played together and was very close, but I wanted to be older. For a while there, my dad was worried I would work those old horses to death.

I used to do the wrangling of a morning as soon as I was old enough. That means taking a saddle horse out to get the other horses you need for the day. The work horses were running south of the house in a three or four hundred acre pasture we called Cherry Draw, and it was my job to get them in by breakfast time. It's rough in the canyons, and you have to get out early to find the horses, but when you are wrangling every day you know the little natural clearings, or parks, where they are likely to be. In June, the wild roses were blooming, and they smelled good in the early morning with the dew on them. So once in a while, when I was ten or eleven, I'd come trotting in at daybreak with fourteen horses and roses in my hat.

I started to school in April of 1918—the spring I was six years old. I remember the first day of school very plainly. My mother and Lucy walked me part way, up to the top of a hill until we were in sight of the schoolhouse, about two miles from home. Then they turned me loose and I went walking on to school by myself.

So my first day of school I went afoot, but I rode a pony later that spring, and we also used horses—either under saddle or hitched to a sled. By the time Lucy and Eugene were going to school, they generally doubled up and rode one horse, and I rode by myself. I was the oldest so I packed more authority.

The Proctor School was built a year or so before I started. For the first two or three years, they had only a seven month term, but then they went to nine. At one time, there were sixteen or seventeen kids going there. A few walked, but most of them rode. One kid had two and a half miles to ride, and he rode bareback all winter. His knees just wore the hair off that old one-eyed roan, Indian pony. In the spring when the new hair came in, it changed color where his knees had been. Any color horse will show marks where a saddle sits or a harness rubs, but it's unusual for one to have knee marks. That old kid would hook his lunch sack over his shoulder like a pocketbook, and here he'd come a-flopping to school. He never did ride a saddle.

At first, we had to tie the horses out to fence posts or trees in all kinds of weather, but later on they put up a little barn—kind of an open shed—where we could tie them out of the storm.

Ray, Lucy, and Eugene, with Sleepy hitched to the sled used for driving to and from school.

In winter time, we used an old wood sled with shafts on either side of the horse. I drove the sled and Lucy and Eugene rode on it. It had a buggy seat, and we'd hook up this work mare, Sleepy, and go to school. We didn't have baled hay, so we put hay in a gunny sack, and at noon we fed it to her. We carried our own lunches in tin tobacco boxes. At that time, Prince Albert or Velvet boxes had two handles up over the top, and they made a nice lunch pail. Every kid had one, because most of the dads smoked. You scratched your name on them with a nail. I haven't seen any in years.

When it was real cold, we melted snow for water, but otherwise, two kids were elected to go the half mile to get a pail of water, and everybody wanted to be the ones go because you could get outdoors for a while. It was fun getting the water out of the well. You had to throw a rope down, pack up a little pail, fill the big three-gallon pail, and then carry it back.

Later, in Mrs. Seig's time as teacher, we took turns bringing soup to school. She would warm it up on a kerosene stove with burners, which was pretty modern then. We carried the soup to school in a gallon bucket. It had a lid on it, and you'd tie a gunny sack around it real tight and pack it on a horse—a sack full of soup. Then we'd put it in a big kettle and heat it up. We all had our cups there. We'd have potato soup, vegetable soup, beef soup—you name it. We never even had crackers. If you wanted anything in your soup, you'd bring some bread. By spring, we would get so tired of soup that we couldn't hardly look at it. We were like old cows that had been on hay all winter, and we'd quit eating it. I have eaten all kinds of soup in my time, going to school, and there's a lot of stew I don't like today, because I had too much of it with everything throwed together. But I don't mind beef broth and tomatoes. That was something a boy named Strand used to bring to school. It was fixed by his father, who was a bachelor.

School would take up at nine, and you'd have a fifteen minute recess in the morning, half an hour at noon, and a fifteen minute recess in the afternoon, so you could get out at three-thirty and start for home. You couldn't just come home and play, you had to figure on feeding the cows and horses. When we drove the sled with Sleepy, we had to take care of her, and if Dad was late coming in from town or somewhere, maybe the barns hadn't been cleaned and we would have to do that, and put in the dairy cows.

We generally milked five or six cows in the winter—not as many as in the summer—and took care of the pigs.

We more or less did all the chores. On real bad-weather nights when my dad was home, he would maybe have most of the chores done but the milking, and he'd already have hay in for our horses. My sister and I helped milk at night and again in the morning.

We'd get done by six o'clock on those cold wintry nights, when it would get dark around four-thirty. The teachers didn't send much homework. I was not much of a student anyway, and when you had to travel out in the cold and come home and do chores, you didn't have time for homework after everything was straightened up.

During the bad winter of 1919, my dad took me to school every day with a team and sled, sometimes dragging a log behind to break a trail so I could walk home. Now and then he'd come for me with a saddle horse, and I'd ride behind him. Mr. Cheek was our teacher then. Teachers were hard to get in them way out places, but he had taken a homestead at Gillette near a friend of his, Judge Irvin. They boarded at the same place and taught schools each way—one at the Proctor School and one at Rocky Crossing.

We had fun that winter because they would conduct mock trials to convict horse and cow thieves. They'd get a bunch of kids together from both schools, and get this trial set up, and somebody would be the thief. There'd be witnesses for both sides, and some kids would be the lawyers, and one kid would be the judge listening to the case. People would come with bobsleds and teams to hear these trials. I was on the jury. I was a pretty small kid and didn't know what I was doing, but we had big times.

The teacher after Mr. Cheek was Gladys LaMay. I got so I just hated arithmetic. She couldn't explain fractions and long division, and she used to get mad at me and bawl me out. Some teachers can explain things so you can go along with it, and with others you can never understand how they want it. So I didn't like Mrs. LaMay, and one day I throwed a spit wad when she was up at the board—and it hit right in front of her. She turned around and caught me because I didn't get my hand back quick enough. She came back and was going to slap me, but I was tall and slim, and the desks were not fastened to the floor, so I just held the desk up in front of me. She'd slap at me, and I'd dodge, and she couldn't get close enough.

I was in the fourth or fifth grade and about the right age to be ornery, and I thought I had it made. But Mrs. LaMay rode to school horseback, and the next day she brought this shot-loaded riding quirt, about three feet long, and hid it in her desk. I got to raising Cain again, and the kids were all laughing about what a show I put on when she couldn't slap me. So she came walking back with her hand behind her, and I thought she was going to slap me again, so I gets all my defenses up and she jerked that quirt out. She could reach me over the shoulders with it, and after about two licks, I gave up. So she stopped that nonsense on my part.

I didn't get into any more trouble except having to stay in after school or having to miss recess. I never had trouble with Mrs. Seig, who came after. She moved into a house near us with her own two kids, and I went to her until I quit school after the eighth grade. I liked arithmetic better with her, because she made it fun and more like a game. She was a real good teacher and was good in the neighborhood. Her kids were in the school, too, and one time her daughter, Mildred, and Ruth Proctor got into a fight with their lunch boxes. We were driving a team and sled home, and we heard a lot of cussing and banging, and it was Ruth and Mildred—or Mutt, as we called her—swinging and batting each other over the head, bending their lunch pails up because they were pretty thin tin.

Another time, Mutt was supposed to go home and stay all night with us, and my sister and brother were on one horse, so Mutt got on behind me on Sleepy. I didn't want her to ride with me—the bigger boys made fun of that—and I was afraid this old mare would throw us both off. But Mutt was brave, so she gets in the saddle, and I'm riding behind the saddle, and half way home something ticked off the old mare. She was goosey from having the two of us on, and she bucked both of us off right over her head. Mutt went off first and I came next. It was a loblolly of mud in the spring of the year, and Mutt had on great big overshoes that weren't buckled. When she got throwed up in the air, her feet flopped, and away they went—one overshoe in each direction.

For fun, at school, we'd play Ante. You'd choose up sides and run around the schoolhouse throwing a ball, and if you hit somebody, he was on your side. And every once in a while, crash!; you'd get a window. Then, when fresh snow came, we played Fox and Geese, or sometimes we'd drag sleds off a saddle horse.

Another winter pastime was sledding down a little hill. We'd get so wet we'd have to come in and sit by the stove. We'd build snowmen and run our sleds into them, and when you hit a snowman with your sled, it would be soft and fly in every direction. But one time when I got to school early, I had time to run out on the sledding hill, and I hit this snowman that had set all night and froze solid. When I hit it, the sled jumped up in the air and throwed me over backward. It's lucky I had my head way up, because if I'd had my head down I might have been killed.

It was kind of rough country with pine trees and rocks and all. We'd build small houses or forts, and pile up lots of pine cones, and have a battle throwing them. They were sharp and sticky, and someone would get hit and start bawling, and the teacher would make us come in, and we couldn't have a pine cone fight for a while. It's a wonder somebody didn't get an eye knocked out.

You didn't have no playground stuff, so you made your own entertainment. We did have a teeter-totter—a long board over a stump—and you'd get a kid on each side and get to going up and down, but somebody would generally get throwed off. We used to play baseball, too. We had an old club of a bat, and we'd choose up sides and then get into a fight over who was out and who wasn't. And we played Ape. We'd crawl up in the pine trees, and somebody was "it" and would come climbing up after you. We'd crawl around and tear our clothes and get our mothers mad at us. If you could get a pine tree that was right limber, you could bend it down and get into another tree, but if it happened to break, you'd fall on your head. There was kids all over the trees, and it's a wonder somebody wasn't killed.

At Halloween, we colored up some paper and put pumpkins and black cats on the windows, and at Halloween and Christmas the teachers would have "dialogues" as they were called—little plays in which all the kids had a part. Of course, the parents would be there for the schoolhouse plays. Once, when I was in the seventh grade, my dad was driving us back from the Halloween play down this old washed out road, and the horses got up on the side in the dark, and the two wheels up on the bank ran over a log, and over went the buggy. My mother and all of us fell out. Some guys come along on horseback and got us straightened up and back on the road.

There were dances, too. One I remember very plainly was on a second of February—Ground Hog Day. It was at a neighbor's who lived three or four miles down off the divide. The snow was deep, but it was thawing and water was running everywhere. We went off over the divide before dark. My mother rode sidesaddle, and my sister and brother were on double, and I was on a little horse by myself. The trail was steep, and as we went riding in down there, big, black clouds rolled in, and it looked like it was going to storm. A little after dark, it started snowing and blowing.

Lots of people had come in buggies and sleds, some thirty-five or forty in all, and they danced and played cards until daylight. I was ten or eleven, and I was dancing some at that age. Some of the small boys used to dance together because there weren't enough girls to go around. There seemed to be all boys in the country and no girls. Now it's just the opposite.

By morning, there was three feet of snow on the ground. They got breakfast for everybody, and I can see yet how the men went to shoveling out gates and getting the horses dug out and sleds uncovered. We saddled our horses and took off for home. Dad went ahead to break a trail. Nowadays, with a car, you would have been there 'til they plowed out the roads, but then it was all horses, so we just broke out a trail and wallowed up onto the divide. When we got home by ten-thirty or so, Dad had to do the chores, but us kids had been up all night so we went to bed.

When I was pretty near to being graduated from eighth grade, we were all at school one day, singing around the stove because it was cold. Dick Proctor was about my size, but a year older, and he wasn't singing. He had been eating beans and he was having trouble with his gas. He was just standing there holding himself. I couldn't resist—I goosed him, and the noise he made sounded like a .30-30. He punched me in the nose and staggered me back a little, but Mrs. Seig just gave us a talking to. I guess she knew what was going on.

Graduation day at Proctor School: Richard Proctor, Ray Holmes, John Davidson, and teacher, Mrs. Lena Seig.

The last year of school we all went out and got little trees to plant in the school yard for Arbor Day. We probably planted cedars or cottonwoods or aspens, because pines are hard to grow, but each kid had his own little tree. We set them out and put stakes over them so people wouldn't walk on them. And in the summer of 1979, I went by there, and there was a broken-off little cedar that had never grown very big, and an aspen tree. So only two of them lived out of thirteen or fourteen trees we had planted fifty years before.

The Proctor School shut down around 1932 after about fifteen years use. After that, kids went to Rocky Crossing where, later on, my sister taught. But the old Proctor School still stands there. I quit school after the eighth grade. You would take exams that had to go back to the County Superintendant's office, and they'd send out your grades from there. I got a hundred on my agriculture test, and passed the rest, but I would have done better if I'd been able to settle down. The trouble was I could always see something on the outside to do and think about—anything but school. When the weather got nice, I had a lot of other projects going, like riding or driving a team. And I liked horse books. *Black Beauty* was my favorite. My folks read it to me, and then I read it myself, and I read it to my kids I don't know how many times. I knew what was ahead in the story, but I enjoyed it every time. Sleepy, that mare that would take us back and forth to school, always reminded me of Black Beauty because she was a wonderful animal. And *Smoky The Cowhorse* was another good book. I still like to read the life of horses.

After I graduated, Mrs. Seig had a ninth grade course at the country school, and I went from September until up in March when I got the measles. I was at a country dance one night, the kind of dance they used to call a "kitchen sweat," and there was a little boy there getting sick. I held him on my lap and talked to him, and I caught the measles. It left me with weak eyes. They bothered me a lot for six months or so, and I wore colored glasses, but I couldn't study, so I quit, and that was the end of my high school education.

I never considered going into Hulett to high school. In those times, you could get a cabin in town and batch, but my folks didn't have the money. And I didn't want to go, so nobody pushed it.

My idol when I was a kid was Tex Martin, an LA Ranch cowboy whose homestead was down the southeast trail off the divide where we lived. His wife stayed down there in the winter alone with the kids, because Tex would be out working. He used to ride in to his family from forty miles away every month or six weeks, going right by our place. He was a big man—about 6′2″—with dark hair and eyes. He wore batwing chaps and heavy rowelled spurs, and he rode a big, snorty, long-legged horse named Darky. Tex was a goer and everybody liked him.

On cold winter days, Tex would come in and put his horse in the barn, and you'd hear him walking in. He wore them spurs over his overshoes, and you'd hear them going r-rrring! He'd throw his spurs in the corner and set down and tell roundup stories.

He started out as a little kid in Deadwood, South Dakota. L.A. Brown owned the LA Ranch—a big outfit at one time—and he saw Tex one day driving a two-wheel cart with a burro hauling rock for some stone building. Brown watched that kid come down with the burro and unload the few rocks he could haul, and go back and get some more, for ten cents a load. Of course, in those times they did things in a slow way.

Tex was a dark little devil who looked like a Mexican, and L.A. Brown thought, "Well, there's one that would make a good hand," so he asked him how he'd like to go out on a roundup. He bought him a bedroll and a $40 saddle, and the kid went right along with him, and he took him out and taught him to be a horse wrangler. From being a horse wrangler, he went to following the roundup wagons through the years, and when there were no wagons anymore, he worked different places as a ranch manager.

So Tex took up a homestead and raised a family near us. He wasn't much of a farmer. He'd put in a little grain and then go out punching cows, or branding calves and working with different outfits. When his kids had to go to high school, he moved them into Spearfish, South Dakota, and started working for the LA again. His wife died of appendicitis before they could get her to the doctor, so the kids grew up kind of here, there, and yonder. One girl still lives in Miles City, and his three sons never went very far. None of them was a cowpuncher. One of them was a natural-born crook who finally died in the penitentiary.

Tex used to like to drink whiskey and get kind of happy. My dad always said he wished somebody could write a book on Tex Martin because he had so many cowpuncher stories. When he came through home the first time, I was seven years old, and I was around him pretty much up to when I was fifteen, although I never worked with him.

He went up to Gillette to work for the Stock Association as deputy sheriff and brand inspector. He caught three guys in Moorcroft one time. When he inspected them, they had too many cattle for the bill of sale, so he arrested them all right there. One of them said, "God-dam it, Tex, you ought to let us go. You stole a lot of cattle in *your* time." Which he had. And he said, "Yeah, but nobody ever caught me!" He had branded slick cattle all right, and they said he made a fortune with cattle on the open range—cattle that didn't cost him anything to run. But when he got to town he gambled and spent his money. Finally, he was elected sheriff for two terms, and then he got so old he had to quit working. He got in a car wreck at the last, and got all broke up, and died in a nursing home.

He was probably forty years old when I first remember him, and really active. He'd come a-riding in on cold days with those spurs jingling. I can just see him now. He was a great visitor and entertainer, and I always dreamed about being a cowpuncher from hearing him tell stories. He was a great guy, and he had a lot of history he could have repeated. But nobody ever wrote a book about Tex Martin.

CHAPTER FIVE

SOME TALK ABOUT WORKING WITH CATTLE

When cows run free, they go more the way nature intended. When they're shut up, they're under stress. Cattle can get used to being shut up, but that way you get more sickness. In big pastures, they can find their own windbreaks, but in small quarters, they've got to stay put. If the wind comes from a bad direction, they can't get out of it. They just have to stand and weather the storm.

Cows are smart up to a point. They know when storms are coming. If it's subzero weather, they'll pull off these creeks here and go to the high ground where it's warmer to bed down at night. And if there's not much protection when it's going to blow, they will stay in on a creek bottom out of the wind. They know where the best feed is, and so they're smart enough to take care of themselves if they've got the chance.

Cattle form groups from ten to twenty-five, or even fifty head. There's generally a lead cow that they follow. If you've got good lead cows, they scatter the cattle. Whenever cattle stay in a tight bunch, they don't do well. That's the idea of riding—to keep them scattered.

Cows from a different country don't move out for grass like the old native cows. They don't know where the grass and the windbreaks are, so they stay along the creeks. I think that falls true about any kind of cattle.

Ray Holmes with Diamond Cross cattle.

They've got to learn the range. Strange cattle don't know the trails up the mountains the way heifers do that've been going up the mountains since they were calves. They are harder to drive, and they don't spread out on the mountain. These fellows that ride on cattle prefer the native cattle that know where the grass is. When they start out, the cattle know where they're going.

Cattle learn a lot from other cattle, and, of course, instinct shows them a lot, too. I'd say it's about a fifty-fifty deal.

You learn through the years to work cattle slow and easy. People that don't know better go to whooping and hollering and whipping and slashing. There is a time to holler at cattle and a time to be quiet. If you're not stirring them up, they are not hard to hold. It's when you got too many people around that the cattle get nervous and want to get away. Of course, there is days that cattle just don't hold. If the wind's blowing and everything, they don't hold—especially if heel flies are working on them. That makes them restless, and they want to run. Once they get riled up, you don't have power enough to hold them.

If you can get cattle to line out and walk so they have plenty of room, the calves will stay up in the bunch. If there are six riders with, say, 150 head, you put two riders up toward the lead. They keep the cattle pointed and strung out. Then two riders would be back with the flank, and two more onto the drags back at the end. The drag drivers should keep track of how the cattle are traveling up in the lead—make the drags walk up a little, or let them drop back giving the bunch room to string out.

That's the trouble nowadays, too many riders get on the back end and keep pushing and the herd gets wider and wider, and pretty soon you are driving them all in a ball. Inexperienced riders will push them too tight together. When you get them bunched up tight, and push them hard trying to move them faster, they bump each other, and the calves automatically get behind and begin bawling for their mothers. Then the mothers turn back to find them. Whenever cattle tighten up into a ball, the calves fall to the back end, and when the riders ride up to try to make the cows go ahead, the calves turn back and run off. When you ride by a calf, and he turns around and don't see his mother, he'll get scared and run.

If the cows are not being pushed too hard and they've got slack, a cow can walk up in the lead for awhile and discover her calf ain't there, and she can come back looking through the bunch, and find him. But if they're all in a tight wad, she don't get a chance. When they get so thick I can't tell if there's a cow and a calf wrong, I shut a gate on them and go on with the main bunch. Then I'll go another day and move some more. If you've got 150 head to go, why you can get out with fifty or sixty head of them in straight pairs, so you've cut the number down. Then maybe you'll go in the evening and get twenty-five or thirty. You just try to work through and pick up what you know is paired, that is, mothered up.

When cattle don't know where they're going, you need more riders up front to keep the lead going. And the guys behind have always got to watch the lead, walking, because the lead's got to go before the back end. Like I said, if everybody pushes from behind, and nobody's pushing up front, the cows jam up because no matter how you try, you can't string them out if the back end is coming too fast.

Working cows is something you learn as you get older, and you have to figure out your own method.

I can work cattle alone under the right conditions. I get twenty-five or thirty head up in the corner of a field, and set there on my horse until they all get quiet, and then ease back a few pairs or some strays. Working alone makes you figure things out, and I learned all this by myself. A lot more people ought to have to work alone, because they'd find out that if you get wild, you ain't going to get it done by yourself. A lot of guys can't do it by themselves because they get impatient and get mad.

You've just got to take your time, and mosey around, even if you might be a long time getting the job done. You sure can't do nothing by getting mad.

I've seen guys that's roping go to dragging and fighting the cows, and they'll fight their horses as well. All they're doing is wearing on their bodies. Christ, horses and cows has got to know what you're whipping them for. It's like with people, if there's two people mad, they never settled an argument. I get mad all right, but there's no use to getting mad at a cow.

When I move cattle alone, I'll be out when it's just starting to break daylight and the cows is just starting to get up. Before the calves nurse is when the cows have their calves with them, so when they drift down the draws, the calves are in the bunch. And it's cool. Cows want to walk early in the morning, and you can get out and make good time with them. When it gets hot, they don't mother up like they do at dawn when the calf wants to suck. In the middle of the day, they are scattered all over. One babysitter cow may be looking after three or four calves, whose mothers are off in the hills underneath the sagebrush or in the draws.

I don't know how they decide which cow is to babysit, but that's what they do. You can see it at calving time, too. There'll be a cow or two that mothers the whole bunch. The others are off grazing or have gone to water. The babysitter cow can more or less hold off coyotes. A coyote can come running along and spook and kill a little calf that's all by itself, but if there's a cow there, why coyotes will generally back away.

So the early morning is the best time to move cows and calves, because you can get them started and know they are pretty straight. In the evening, they generally mother up again when they bed down at night, but you don't have much time to work between the time it gets cool and the time it gets dark.

I start the cows and calves slow and let the calves follow their mothers, and I don't bunch them up too much. There's generally a lead cow, and I keep the lead strung out, and the cows know more or less where they're going. I follow them along slow, and they graze and eat, and the calves follow along. It takes quite a while to do that. With some help, you could go faster. Alone, it takes a lot of time and patience, but when I get to doing something like that, it's fun to me, and I don't think too much about it. I let the cattle mosey along, and go their own way, and they don't get excited or run off.

But working alone makes a lot of extra riding. You have to ride up to turn the lead, and then ride back to the drags and push them up, so you cover lots more miles than if you had some help. You about double the amount of riding, and it uses up your horse. I always figured it was kind of a glory to myself to get some job done alone that usually takes more than one person. I have done that many a time. This girl once said she wanted to come along to see how I worked cattle by myself, but I told her, "If you was along, I wouldn't be by myself!"

Dogs are all the fashion today, but I don't need dogs for trailing cattle. If a dog would learn how to get up and take the lead cattle and go on, that would be the place for him. But the dogs I've seen can't do that.

If a dog was trained to stay behind your horse, or stay farther back, that would be fine. Usually, they run right up behind a bunch of cows, nip them, and start them running so the back end of the bunch tries to outrun the lead. Any bunch of cattle most generally wants to move. The cows don't mind people on horseback, but when they are walking along with their calves and a dog comes up, they start fighting the dog. And if a dog happens to bite a calf, that calf'll beller and all the other cows turn around to protect their own calves.

If you were going to work cattle in a fence corner by yourself, you'd find cows would go up naturally into a little bunch and hold pretty well. But when there is a dog around, they get all excited. You have to have them quiet when they are mothering up.

Up to a point, trained dogs can be helpful scaring dry cattle and slow cows off the hillsides and bringing them down. They can be really good for riling steers and getting them out of the brush. A good trained dog in rough country can run and nip a cow, and start her down a creek, and then the other cows'll loosen up. So long as you don't dog them too much, cattle won't turn around and fight.

But I don't want a dog even in the brush. I'm my own dog, and I've got my own tricks. You can't do much with cows afoot, and that ain't cowboy stuff, anyway, but when there's no way to get a horse in somewhere, you can start cows going afoot if they're kind of spooky. If it's real muddy, you can jump off and run in and boo them, and jump them out of the brush. I can tread that soft mud real fast, and I don't put much weight on either foot. You can learn to travel light on your feet and keep moving. I've seen guys that go into mud knee deep, and it can get soft enough that I go in. But if I get the right speed up, and get my feet to going, I can stay on top and get across. You've got to travel fast and keep your feet flying!

If cattle get down somewhere where I can't get them, sometimes I'll throw rocks at them. And if a bull gets over a bank, and just stands there in the brush, I throw a rock on top of him, and that'll bring him out. So when I'm moving cattle I'll do about anything to keep them going, or to get them out of the brush—from using tin cans on up. There's already one hole in a beer can, so you can poke another hole and string twelve or fourteen cans on a wire. When you shake it, it rattles, and if cattle ain't used to it, why they booger and get going. They can't figure what that noise is. Cattle is spooked of a strange noise.

We used to call the beer-can rattles "Mexican sheep-dogs," because the Mexicans used them to move lambs. When lambs are little, and guys are trying to put them in a pen to shear, the lambs get to running back, and you can rattle at them and it spooks them and keeps them up among the sheep.

I brought a Mexican steer out of thick brush that way one time—a steer I couldn't get otherwise. I'd ride over to get him, and run him out of one brush patch, and before I could get back on my horse, he'd walk down in the brush again and look at me. One morning he went in there and was standing, so I rode up to him and set there a little bit. I only had one beer can with some rocks in it, but I rattled that beer can and, God, he just come out of that brush and run up the hillside and started up the road.

He got up towards the gate I wanted to get him through, but I didn't know how to get off and get the gate open without him running off. That steer went up to a fence corner, and I was wondering what to do with him, so I thought, well, I'll just rattle once more to see if he will jump—and he jumped clear over into the cows.

I sometimes take a blacksnake whip along on my horse, and if cows are going kind of slow or thinking about turning back, I can reach out with that whip and hit one at the right time. That scares a cow, and she'll go straight ahead instead of turning back. Or if a cow wants to come by you out of the herd, you can sometimes throw that whip out there to turn them back. It's the noise that does it; it doesn't hurt them.

An old cow learns to respect a whip. If she goes walking by and gets hit a time or two, she'll respect that she better not come by you. Sometimes I use my rope the same way, to whack an animal and make him go. You can make a calf follow a cow that way, too. Sometimes you're driving out a cow, and the calf is just sauntering along, and you can peck him with a rope. It'll scare him and he'll get up with his mother and keep going.

I really like whips. They're nice to have around, although some people are always whacking and hitting with them. I only use them when it'll do some good. When you're trailing cattle, there's no use in riding up on them with a whip when they ain't got any place to go. The back end of the bunch can only go when the leaders go. But whips are handy with a lead bunch of cattle when they're weaving around. You get that whip down and get them a little excited, and they'll think about hitting the trail.

So you can work whips a lot of different ways, but there's times to whip cows and times not to. You've got to spend a lot of years before you figure it all out.

"Making a circle" is when you're gathering cattle off a big, open range and bringing them in to a central point. The riders are placed around so they can cover the country and still come back into the central location. You start a couple of guys off on a shorter circle to bring in what they can find. They don't have to go so far to get their cattle down to the central point, so they'll be there when more cattle start coming out of the hills. They'll be able to hold them up, so they don't go on down country.

The last man off they call the circle leader. He's got the longest circle to make. It takes him quite a while to get in with his cattle, but the others keep coming in ahead of him and everybody is holding the herd.

"Rawhiding" is something different, a cleaning up project, gathering anything that got missed. It can take a good number of riders, but where I've worked, it's most generally been me.

Getting cattle through gates can be a problem. Sometimes when you bring a cow to a gate she'll go through, but if you come agalloping right up on a bunch, and they don't know there's a hole in the fence, they'll run back. You've got to have them looking to see a place to go without getting excited. When their heads are in the air and they are running, they don't see nothing.

Crossing water is another problem. You drive cows down to the water, and they'll try to break back, so you keep turning them. If you keep turning them, and not getting them too excited, just keep turning them in, after a while they'll be standing in a bunch. After they've been turned back so many times, they think there's no use to run back anymore, so they'll start going where you want them to—even across the water. You have to give them time to look everything over, because if you ride into them, and get them all excited, they'll split to the four winds.

On a bridge, it's better for two riders to be up ahead getting the lead started. You keep the cows funneling in and keep them pushing right up against one another. When one looks down and sees it's a bridge, why they can break in the middle, and then you have to get another lead. To keep cattle coming right on, they've got to have a lead.

Trailing uphill is something else. You want to get your lead cattle started up high on the hill and keep them up high. You've got to keep them pushed up all the time to make them climb a hill, because they have a tendency to swing down. If they get down too low, then you can't work them back up. My theory is to put your riders on the lower side, and hold the cows up towards the trail as high as you can, depending on the grade.

You have to keep cattle more strung out in the mountains than on the prairie, because up on the mountain trails, if you're inexperienced, you can get your cattle in a jam before you know it. Inexperienced riders have no idea how to go through timber, or over downed trees, or how to get around to turn cattle. They just follow the cows, and pretty soon the cows are all gone. There's probably some mountain riders still, but it's hard to find ones that know what to do.

In timber, you don't just pick up a bunch of cattle and go. On a prairie or in open country, a bunch can be wider and more spread out, because you can see where they are going. But in the timber and in the mountains, you can't see the cows behind you, and you can't mother up your cattle. You have to pick up and go with what cattle you have. So you string them out, and you don't try to take too many, and you push them aways and drop them off in a park. Then the calves mother up, and the big percentage of them will stay right there. Anything that's not mothered up will turn back, so the next day you'll pick those up and go on again, working them back to the park with the others. There's a lot more that you've got to think about in the mountains than in open country.

Nowadays there are so many tourists up in the mountains that there's many places you can't take cattle anymore. If you turn cows into parks where there are trailers and dogs and stuff, the cattle will pull out. I haven't done any riding up there in years, but I know the tourists have created a problem. When people are around on foot, they spook cattle out of the area they are running in.

The whole country has settled up now, and people don't want you crossing their grass. What grass they have is fenced up in fields, so it's pretty near impossible to get through. People are not used to letting you trail across, and if you have a couple hundred head of cattle, it takes room to get through. Most likely, nobody wants to let you in on water, so you pretty near have to trail on the county road.

In earlier days, once the railroads were all over the country, you trailed the cattle three or four days and loaded them on the train. Cattle are moved mostly by trucks now, and when they are loaded out, they are pushed fast. But whenever you move cattle too fast and hurry them around, that causes them to shrink and lose weight. My idea is to walk them in natural and not be in too much hurry. Of course, there is times when you are corralling cattle when you are better to spook them right along and get them in the corral. Even if you come slow, you can have a hard time corralling them, and when they get to milling, that causes shrink, too.

There is a time to hurry and a time not to.

When you get cows and calves into the corral for weaning, you cut off the calves. That means letting the cows go out one way and the calves the other. That's the last time they'll see each other. If you are working with a good crew, you can cut them off pretty fast. Somebody will get in the corral, and you leave one man on the gate, either on horseback or on foot. Then you start the cows towards the gate. They start trailing, and you just let the cows by and spook the calves back. If the calves are not scared from behind, they will not run over you to get out the gate. They will kind of hesitate because they are timid. So that's what's called cutting off the calves.

If you are sexing them, you can mother them up on the outside—steers and their mothers in one pasture, and heifers and their mothers in a different pasture. Then when you bring them in, all you have to do is cut off the calves and they are ready to load.

When you are working a herd, there's a rule that you don't ride between another man and the cattle. Say he was bringing a cow out and you was following, you would not ride between the cow and his horse. Or if he's going back into the herd after a cow, you wouldn't ride in front of him. Even just holding a cut, you don't ride in front of someone else.

When I am working cattle alone, with nobody to hold them up for me while I am cutting, of course they can run off. What I do is get my cattle stopped and quiet, and set on my horse, and turn back the cows I don't want out. If you want a cow or two out of the bunch, you can make the right jump with your horse at the right time and not scare the other cattle. But the bunch has to be standing kind of quiet. You kind of let them work themselves. Then, when you see an opening, you take advantage of it and get the cows you want cut off.

It takes time and patience. After a while, maybe you don't even jump your horse. You set there and let the cows mill around and around, and pretty soon the one you want will come out on the edge, and you can cut her off and put her where you want her.

You have to be quick-witted to deal with livestock—more so than to be a farmer, because so much comes up on the spur of the moment. When you go out to farm, maybe to put in some kind of grain, you have more time to think about what you are doing. With livestock, things happen all of a sudden, and you have to have fast reflexes. Some people can't think fast enough to keep ahead. You have to be smarter than the cow.

But those are all things you figure out as time goes by. The more you work with livestock, the more you know, and you still don't know it all if you live a thousand years. There's still a few smart guys working with cattle, but they don't have the chance to get enough experience. I worked in hard times, and I got chewed out and stayed on, but you was either going to work or go hungry—whichever paid the best! In my time, ranch work was the only steady job there was. Other jobs didn't amount to anything, and they didn't last long. It was nothing like it is today. Nowadays, if a guy gets disgusted, he can quit and, hell, the next day he's still eating. The government'll pay him.

CHAPTER SIX

THE DEPRESSION YEARS (1928–1937)

In 1928, I worked mostly at home. I helped the neighbors and did odd jobs, because those were good years and we did some farming. Then in 1929, it turned a little dry and I helped my dad threshing, doing some riding, and a little bit of everything. That was the year of the big crash on Wall Street, and then prices came down and it began to get tough to get jobs.

I never really had a steady job at that time. I would ride a horse for somebody for five dollars, or go out and help a neighbor for a day or two. I just drifted around clear through the Depression until 1934, when I went to work for Winnie Richards. So for five years, I just dogged over the country working here and there to make a dollar. I had a few head of cattle that I ran at home, but I sold them for $20 a cow, $15 a yearling, and $10 a calf, so they didn't bring much money.

One job was helping to trail sheep. In 1930 or 1931, I helped trail about 400 lambs from Barlow Canyon to the Bunny ranch at Aladdin. We took a grub box, a skillet, and a team and wagon. One of us would drive the sheep and one of us would drive the team. We had a saddle horse along, and we rode part of the time and walked part of the time. It took two days.

Ray in 1928 on his first horse, Red, with new saddle and bridle.

We'd go as far as Alva the first day and stay overnight. One time in October, when we was sleeping in a hay mow at a barn there, it was storming and the guy I was with looked at his watch and said it was time to get up and get going because it was five o'clock and it would soon be getting light. So we got up and rolled up our bed, and lit our coal-oil lantern, and went out, and built us a bonfire, and cooked our breakfast. We put our beds in the wagon and harnessed our team, but still it didn't come daylight. I looked at my watch, and it was only about one thirty. He'd mistaken twenty-five past twelve for five o'clock. So we had to go pack our beds back in the barn and lay down and go to sleep again. And when it did come five o'clock, boy, it was a-snowing, wet like rain. We didn't cook any breakfast. We just started trailing sheep.

The Bunny place was on Hay Creek, five or six miles north of Aladdin, and we'd generally get there by the next night. They had a Delco plant—the first electric lights I was ever around. In them times, there were no electric freezers or other appliances. Lights was the only thing used. They had a great big barn that held a lot of horses and cows, and a big hay mow. There was a cement floor in it, and when we'd get in there with the electric lights at night, I thought it was the most wonderful thing to see—a ranch all lit up with electric lights!

Then there was the time I went out on a threshing crew. There were six teams that hauled the bundles into the threshing machine, and two teams to haul the grain away with a wagon. There was one cook in a sheep wagon and he cooked for nine men on one little stove.

We had to roll our beds out at night. They had heavy soogans or quilts in them, and wool or cotton blankets. You'd put out a bed tarp on the ground—about seven feet wide and sixteen feet long for a double bed. You'd open the tarp on the ground and put your bed on about half of it, and bring the other part up over the whole bed. You'd pull the tarp clear over your head if it rained.

Well, it stormed and snowed a litle that night. We turned all the work horses loose and throwed the harnesses over the wagon tongues or laid them on the ground. During that first night, some of the horses walked up so close to the beds that a few of the older fellers there were afraid of getting stepped on. I'd gone to bed with everybody else, but then I went and got a set of harness and started rattling the chains that hook onto the wagon, hollering "Whoa! Whoa! Whoa!" Everybody jumped out in the snow barefoot in their underwear thinking a horse was tangled up in some harness and was running over the top of them.

I didn't know if they was going to let me get back in bed or not. It's a wonder they didn't run me off, jumping them out of bed that way in their underwear.

There was always somebody to play a joke. One time in the 1930s at the OW Ranch on Powder River, they were all sitting around in a circle on the ground, and George Benedict killed a bull snake. He put a big safety pin through the tail, and slipped alongside this guy who had his shirttail out, and pinned it on him. When the guy happened to look around, he jumped a little bit, and then looked straight ahead, and then looked back—and took a second look—and the snake moved—and then he went hysterical running and screaming with the snake flopping on his legs. The boss finally got it off him and said if he ever found out who done that he was going to fire him. But nobody ever told.

I worked at a sawmill, too. Sometimes you'd have to take lumber for pay, and then you couldn't sell the lumber. Hell, I got five or six thousand feet of lumber once that I couldn't sell. It was as if you'd worked there and never got any money at all because you couldn't move the lumber.

My dad and his brother Clyde each had a homestead near Devils Tower, and they worked together, but them bad years you couldn't raise anything. In 1930 and the next three years, it just kept getting worse, and you'd have to cut back because every year was a little bit drier, and there were Mormon crickets as big as your thumb. When 1934 came in, it was as bare as out here in the shale. The grass didn't even get green. That was the dust bowl when the Okies all took off and went to California. The cattle had to live on oak leaves or anything they could find. My dad and Uncle Clyde had to get rid of our cattle in 1934. That was the endgate.

The government bought the cattle. It was a good thing Roosevelt put in that program, because you had to pay the freight even before they would put cattle on the train. And if you was in debt to the bank, there was five dollars a head that the bank couldn't touch. It went to the family.

The WPA crews killed the cattle that a vet said was too poor and weak. The government teams killed them and covered them with dirt. It would have been billions of dollars worth of cattle today that were covered over where the interstate goes through now. Sheep were killed the same way. They would shoot anything that was too weak to be shipped out. They skinned them with skinning crews and baled the hides. They could sell the wool. But the cattle would be just a rack of bones.

Anybody who had some money could really come out of it good, because you could buy that land for fifty cents or a dollar an acre. Anybody that got hold of that land, and kept going, starving along with it, was in business when land prices started to rise again. The younger generation that got it, why it's made wealthy people out of them.

Nobody thought about mineral rights. I had an uncle at Moorcroft who came in there as a young feller, and went to barbering, and married my mother's sister. He fooled around trying to raise grain, and had a few cows, and tried to work on the ranch and cut hair. He ran a pool hall and would start barbering about noon and work until midnight if there was anybody there. But he got tired of the ranch and sold it for about a dollar an acre . . . and God, there is oil wells pumping all over that thing now, and he never got a dime.

If your front sight was as good as your hind sight, why you'd really be in the money.

I'd never say I was hungry during the Depression. There was always something off the ranch. Women canned and had their own bacon and flour. If people then had had what they pay just for utilities today, they would have been living high on the hog. My sister, Lucy, got $50 a month for teaching school in Sundance, and she'd go to the store in Spearfish and buy $25 worth of groceries. I remember hauling them boxes and $25 worth of groceries was quite a lot. It practically wintered us, outside of little odds and ends.

In 1932, I stayed with my sister while she was teaching. She didn't like to stay away from home, so I went over before Thanksgiving and figured on being there only a short time, getting wood up for her and doing odd jobs. My sister done all the cooking, because I wasn't a very good cook. We had a room with a heating stove in it, and we had a curtain across for our bedroom part. I would get up in the middle of the night and fix the heating stove: The house wasn't very warm. On real cold nights, the cookstove would go out. I always had a nice lot of kindling, and I'd get up first thing and start the fires, then Lucy would get up and cook breakfast. It was pretty cold that winter through January and February, and many a time the tea kettle would be froze on the stove, and the water bucket, too. We didn't have any cellar there to keep stuff from freezing. It takes quite a lot to freeze canned goods in boxes, but to keep the potatoes from freezing, I used to put them in bed with me at night.

You used to figure on burning about a cord of wood a month in a heating stove. A cord is four foot wide, four foot high, and eight foot long, and it would take two men to cut a cord of wood in a day.

So I got the wood cut for my sister, and the Depression was on, and there wasn't anything to do. You couldn't buy a job. I ended up staying with her until April. I played cards around the neighborhood, and went to a few dances, and had a pretty good winter at that. I didn't make no money, but me and another guy cut five cords of wood for the schoolhouse. We sawed it by hand, hauled it a couple of miles in a wagon, and we got seventy-five cents a cord. That is a lot of work for seventy-five cents. But we was getting exercise.

Nobody knows how tough it was. They talk about no jobs today, but Christ, there is all kinds of jobs. Then, there was lots of guys working for their board, and some couldn't even get a job for their board. If you got fifty cents a day, or worked for your board, you was just surviving. There were hungry people and soup lines. In the big cities, they were starving. Then they started in the relief programs, helping people and putting out public works, but anybody that was single couldn't get a job doing that. You had to be a married man.

So I done a little of everything along the line. I went out and put in a hundred acres of wheat one fall right during the worst drought year. This guy made me a deal that he had the ground and the seed and the horses, and if I got that hundred acres in, he'd furnish my grub and give me a third of the grain the next year. I've forgotten what wheat was at then, maybe twenty-five or thirty cents a bushel, but a dollar looked as big as a wagon wheel. And the next year was so dry the wheat all burned up. So I never got nothing for my wages.

There wasn't much wild game around to hunt at that time. The deer never come in. I was a grown man before I knew what deer meat was. I don't know what happened to the deer population. I suppose people killed a lot of them, but I think there was so many coyotes that they killed off the fawns. But we had hogs and beef. Of course, you could only have beef more or less in the wintertime. With pork, they would butcher the hogs, and render up the lard, and cure it themselves, and hang it in the smoke house, and it would keep all summer. You didn't have to worry about it. It was really good cured meat.

In 1934, I started working more steady. For ten dollars a month, I fed hundred head of cattle and got my board out of it. In the winter of 1935, I worked cutting lumber and posts; 1936 was another bad year, I kind of drifted from job to job over thirty-five or forty miles. I never even had a car at that time. You might spend two weeks here and three or four days there. By 1937, it still wasn't good, but it had started getting a little better.

Prohibition ended in 1933, and I remember when beer came back in. I was in Sundance where this guy had his beer parlor all set up, and he drove to Moorcroft to get a load of beer. He got back about six in the morning, and everybody helped him unload. So he opened up his saloon, and we was drinking legal beer, and oh, how good it was! God, it was nothing but "near" beer, nothing like today, but people were hollering, "We want beer! We want beer!" as they was waiting for that first load to come in.

There was a bar in Hulett that opened in 1934 and has been there ever since. It was run by a Swede, and he used to set in there in a rocking chair with a sheepskin on it, and he'd mix up a big shot of whiskey, and set there and read the paper. Business wasn't too lively in the daytime. He had a pail of water there, and if you bought a straight shot of whiskey, why he would take and dip the glass, after you were done, in that cold water and turn her upside down to dry. If you wanted a little whiskey and water, why he reached out of the same pail and pour it back in for a drink, and you had whiskey and water. I never did see any ice in that bar.

They had the CCC camps then. These boys would come in from the Blue Ridge Mountains, and some of them was so tough that the camp over at the Tower Reserve shipped them back home. They couldn't do nothing with them. Christ, they couldn't read or write, and they'd come out of them hills where they was used to fighting, and they'd be looking for moonshine.

They'd come into that Hulett bar and get drunk. They thought the old Swede was quite a guy. They'd tell him they heard this was tough country and they was wanting to meet some of those cowboys, and he told them, "Well, if the cowboys here was like they used to be, you boys

Post office, Oshoto, Wyoming.

would be six foot under." So they got drunk at this dance and got to falling around, and started a big fight with the local boys. It turned into kind of a riot. The government CCC boys—they was kind of like MPs in the service—had to plunk them on the head with billy clubs to quiet them down, and they loaded them in paddy wagons and took them back to the Tower Reserve.

A lot of people got in trouble. The Swede in Hulett used to sit in his bar on Sunday and read. The door was shut, but it wasn't locked. If you knew about it, you'd just open the door and walk in. He done that for several years until someone reported him. One day when they was building the new highway into Hulett, two men walked in wanting to buy two bottles of beer and a fifth of

Troad Pearson store and bar, Hulett.

whiskey. The Swede said, "Well, I don't believe I know you." They said they were "road men," and he thought they was working on the new road, so he sold them two bottles of beer and a fifth of whiskey. The next morning, the sheriff from Sundance, Blakeman, was over there with a warrant for him. "Them dirty sons of bitches told me they were road men!" he complained, but they fined him, and I suppose he kept the door locked after that. They all laughed about the Swede thinking they was road men working on the road. They was road men, all right, federal revenue men on the road checking on bars that was open on Sunday.

Sheriff Blakeman was my uncle. He wasn't too big a man, about six foot tall, but he was a goer. He was never in the office, because he was out driving over the country looking for thieves or for something wrong. He started as a carpenter, but he studied all the law books, and when he was sheriff he settled a lot of little cases himself. He should have been a lawyer, because he really knew the law. He wasn't afraid of anybody. Today, somebody probably would have shot him.

It was still moonshining time for two years after Blakeman got in. He'd drop in unexpected at a dance where there was moonshine, and the guys would have to cache their bottles. No one ever knew where he was going to show up, because he liked to travel. He generally didn't pay too much attention to moonshine, but people knew if they got rowdy he'd lock them up. He overlooked a lot of it, but if somebody was out of order, he'd whip them.

Blakeman electioneered from little kids on up. When the kids was young, he was giving them candy and doing things for them, so when they got to be twenty-one years old, he had them on his side so they'd vote for him. In World War II, he done a lot for the service boys trying to get home on furlough. They'd maybe get as far as Newcastle and be stranded, and he'd jump in his car and go over there and get them.

Once there was another fellow who run for sheriff. His wife was the one doing the electioneering then, and they was good people, but folks didn't like her. She was a rough-talking old gal, and she talked too much. She come over to Oshoto to get the mail one time, and she was kind of limping, and somebody said to her, "What happened to you, Maggie?" And she said, "Well, I fell down and pretty near broke my back on a frozen cow turd!"

Her husband was a slow, easy-going guy, so she done the talking for him. They drove into Sundance one time, and she says to Blakeman, "Blakeman, I don't want any hard feelings after the election, 'cause we've been all over the county, and my husband is going to win." That was because when he and his wife would drive in somewhere, the folks was saying sure, they'd vote for him.

Well, her husband didn't get many votes, and after the election, Maggie said, "There sure is a lot of goddamned liars in Crook County!"

So Blakeman was sheriff for twenty-four years and went out without being beat. He just got too old and had to give it up.

There was a lot of stories about Prohibition and the years after. Doc Adams was the dentist in Hulett, and he never gave any pain killer when he pulled a tooth. He just snapped his puller on and jerked it out. He was a little frail guy who looked like a chickadee. His legs wasn't much bigger around than my finger. But he could make good store teeth at that time.

Well, there was a traveling man who could never get any teeth to fit him, and he heard about Doc Adams, so he got Doc started on a set of teeth. This fellow went over to Sherm Brimmer, who had the blacksmith shop and garage, and told Sherm, "The old dentist wanted a drink, so I got him a drink of moonshine while he's working on my teeth." Old Sherm said, "Well, that is the end of your teeth!" Doc Adams just got drunk, and the guy had to come back later to get his teeth. Doc Adams never had too much money, and he couldn't get ahold of that moon all the time, so when he got some, he kept right on drinking. In the end, he quit the business and lived to be an old man on welfare.

Then there was Truman Vesser, another uncle of mine, who is dead now. He was drinking pretty bad at that time, and he was supposed to have bleeding ulcers.

He got to drinking a bunch of that red sloe gin, got drunk, fell over, went to vomiting, and they thought he was bleeding to death. They rushed him to the hospital in Gillette, and when they got him up there, the doctor said there wasn't nothing wrong with him. He wasn't bleeding, it was just the sloe gin.

That sloe gin is pretty potent stuff. I could get a bottle of that down to where the label said "sloe," and then it got fast from there on out.

A traveling salesman who had some real good whiskey with him came through Hulett during moonshine days. Troad Pearson was running the store, and this guy said he could get him a fifty-gallon barrel of this whiskey sent down from Canada. All he'd have to do was mark it "vinegar." At that time, in them old country stores, everything was more or less in bulk. So, old Doc Adams and a couple of others that liked to get together for a little poker and moonshine joined in and paid their money down. I don't know how much it cost for a barrel of whiskey, but they all put in their money and waited for this good liquor to come. Sure enough, the barrel came in marked "vinegar," and boy, they tapped it, and it was vinegar! So, that was a swindler that come along and took the boys for a ride. I guess they sold the vinegar.

My first steady job was working for Winnie Richards out by Oshoto, which I started in the fall of 1934. I had been working around at odd jobs when she came with her father-in-law, Irv Richards, to get my dad to help them fix a well. I went out to help him, and they decided to keep me on. Winnie Richard's husband, Delbert, had been killed in a car wreck that July, and they didn't have anybody to work there. I went ahead and stayed there that winter. Oshoto was a fine community; everyone got together on Saturday nights and played cards or maybe danced.

Winnie Richards branded a Z4. The ranch was on the Little Missouri River that flows into the big Missouri. It's flat, open country with lots of sagebrush and a few cottonwood and ash trees along the creek. There were some nice hay meadows and a house, a barn, a garage, an ice house, bunkhouse and chicken house. They built onto the house the year I was there. Two good carpenters worked all summer and got a dollar a day.

I worked there about a year—ranch work with some riding and haying, fencing, milking cows, feeding the hogs and looking after the chickens. In the summer, there were probably a couple hundred head of cattle. At Thanksgiving, Winnie Richards went off to visit her folks, so I had to be there, but after I milked two cows, and took care of my team and two or three horses, I got on this paint stud that we used for a saddle horse and rode home seventeen miles. I had Thanksgiving dinner with my folks and come back the seventeen miles that night, and milked the cows again before I went to bed. It was pretty hard work to go out and do everything that a man has to do on a ranch, even if there ain't much going on. I'd say there was lots of things I learned at Winnie Richard's the hard way.

One thing I learned about was runaways. I was feeding cottonseed cake to the cattle one day—little chunks you scatter out on the ground—and I drove this team up on the hill with the paint stud tied on behind, so I could ride him later to bring in the cows. I'd wrapped up the team lines tight to a stick on the hayrack, and the team was standing there, and I was scattering cake to the cows, when a bunch of loose horses came running over the hill and scared the team.

Off they ran with the paint stud tied on behind, but he didn't leave as fast as they was running, and pretty soon he fell down. It was level sagebrush country with some little dips across, nothing big, just little ditches, and they drug that stud 'til finally he broke the rope. He stayed right there, so I got ahold of him, and jumped on, and swung the team around against a fence. By that time, they was getting run down. I was lucky that time. Nothing got broke or tore up, and the stud (we called him Paint) had a little hide knocked off of him, but he was all right.

Another time, I wasn't so lucky with a runaway. I had four rollicky horses hooked up to an empty wagon. They hadn't been worked in a long time, and they was full of fire and vim and vigor. I'd set a can of cream in the wagon and headed down a grade to the mailbox. An empty wagon is easy to pull of course, and this lead team is charging along trotting down the road, tugs a-flopping. Then, an outside snap on the one horse's line come loose. When I pulled the line, I couldn't stop the horse. He knew something was wrong. So I hollered "Whoa," and thought I could pull them up. The wheel team was gentle, and when I said "Whoa," the wheel team pulled up, but the lead team came around and jackknifed the wagon. That throwed the can of cream out, and throwed me off the spring seat, and the wheel team got scared, and they all ran off across the country, wide open. When they come to a tree, the leaders swung out and went around, but the wheel team couldn't make the turn, so they spread out and the wagon hit the tree with such force that it jerked the horses back, and they came to a dead stop. I goes down and unhooks them all from where they're tied up, but the cream is spilled, and the outfit's wrecked, and it takes all day to put it right. I made a lot of points with that widow woman!

I spent the winter of 1935–1936 at the Frisbies's ranch. They had an old–time ranch house and I slept upstairs. It took a lot of wood to keep it warm, and we had to pump the water and pack it in. Mrs. Frisbie was a real ranch cook, and we had lots of good grub to eat even if the times was hard—plenty of meat and everything.

It was real warm upstairs where I slept, because the old floor wasn't tight. You could look down and see the lights through the floor. Mrs. Frisbie used to set up half the night to keep wood fires going for the flowers. She had the prettiest geraniums you ever saw, and they bloomed all winter.

The Frisbies didn't have much money and only fifty head of cows to feed. That winter it was so cold some days you couldn't even saw wood. I was there all winter, but from the first of the year, I never got over a month's wages. You couldn't do anything, and the Frisbies couldn't keep me around except for my board.

There was a dance about the first of the year—the kind they called a "kitchen sweat" because they danced in the kitchen. Everybody would come to the dances, maybe thirty or thirty-five people, and there wasn't much room. The ladies would bring pie or cake and sandwiches, and whoever held the dance made coffee. They'd have somebody play the violin, and somebody on the guitar or accordion, and you'd take up a collection for the musicians who got five bucks or, if they was lucky, seven and a half or ten, depending on the crowd.

Everybody thought they ought to have a little whiskey for the "kitchen sweat" that was coming up that Saturday, but the snow was real deep, and of course you couldn't get around in cars because there was no four-wheel drive. Jim Frisbie decided he needed a barrel of gasoline to saw wood, so he sent me to town on Wednesday or Thursday, and everybody chipped in for whiskey. We put hay in a bob sled, and I drove to Hulett and got a barrel of gas, and then drove up to the saloon, and I think I bought fifteen pints. We laid it in under the hay in the sled and never took it out. When the dance got going, and people began getting drunk, the women couldn't figure out where the whiskey was coming from.

I cached a pint in a big snow bank close to the house, and put a boot track over it so I'd know where it was, but people made so many tracks that we had to get out the scoop shovels to find the whiskey. Everybody was out digging snow.

I was feeling kind of foolish, and I went up and asked one girl if she'd like to dance. When she said, "yes," and got up, I said, "I didn't want to dance with you, I just wanted to try out asking you." She sat down. I didn't know her very good, and she never was very friendly after that.

After a while, everybody sobered up because they run out of whiskey, but one guy kept wanting to drink. There was a cream separator on the porch, and it had separator oil in it which is very thin and light colored. "Here's a drink!" he shouted and took a big shot, and then spit oil all over the side of the building.

Nineteen thirty–six was an awful dry year when I didn't find much to do. There wasn't nothing but grasshoppers and crickets, and nothing to do at home. I helped out my grandmother and Mel Storms a little for my board. They had a small place and a hundred head of cows. We'd get up a little wood and listen to the radio and fool around. I throwed a lot of good years away that I wasn't making any money, but nobody was making any money.

That winter, I helped some neighbors put up ice and kind of fooled over the country. One time, I fell in getting ice. I was with my dad and a man by the name of Earl Franklin. When you go to pull out a block of ice, you'd have a little foothold where you put your heel so you wouldn't slip. Well, my foot slipped as I was jerking that block, and I shot down into the water hole that was about six feet deep. I was wearing bib overalls and didn't go out of sight, so Earl Franklin was able to hook onto me with the ice tongs and jerked me back out.

I had to ride five miles home. It was subzero weather, and my clothes went to freezing. My overalls iced over, and when they froze solid they rattled just like boards. I was chilly when I got home, but it wasn't as cold as you'd think, because frozen over like that, there's no wind comes in your underwear. I had to stand around a stove and thaw my overalls loose to get them off. My mother was there and got these clothes off me, and I got in the old wash tub for a hot bath. I didn't even catch cold.

The first part of 1937, I worked up to Alzada, Montana, on a gravel job driving a truck. There was four of us. Two of us worked nights and two worked days. We worked eight hour shifts and got fifty cents an hour, or four dollars a day. It cost us a dollar a day board at the mess hall.

The haulers didn't think they was getting enough money, so they decided one night they'd pull a strike. They shut everything down, and it was kind of exciting that night with everyone sitting around drinking whiskey, and talking about hanging the bosses, and running them Cats over the bank—which they might have done—and one thing and another. Ten or twelve of us went to breakfast that morning, and the company outfit that was boarding the men told us "no work, no grub," and they wouldn't let us have breakfast. There was a lot of men in this big bunk house, and everybody got together and went over and told them they was going to tear that cook shack apart if they didn't feed us. So, the boss told them to feed us, because we was still paying for board.

Finally the sheriff, my uncle Bill Blakeman, come over and talked with the truck drivers and the company men, and we ended up getting more money for hauling gravel. But the company found other ways to gyp us. For instance, they wouldn't give you a full load on your truck. The guy would open up and let the load he wanted to into your truck, and you'd have no way to check it out when they motioned to you to get moving. It was a long haul to where we was going, and they'd weigh the load when we got there, and you got paid by the ton, and you might find you was a thousand pounds short. So, we got gypped all the way through.

After the strike, four of us figured we'd batch on our own. We went into town, got this sheepwagon, put it on a truck, and set it flat on the ground without the wheels. It was equipped with cupboards and everything, so the four of us put our bucks together and got a lot of groceries. One day the wind blowed so damned hard the company pulled all the trucks off, so we went up to Alzada and got two quarts of Bluebird gin, and mixed it up with lemon juice, and went fishing. We couldn't catch nothing except big turtles, so we come home. We had some beans stewing on the stove, and some raisins—I was baking a pie. I reached over to get the raisins and throwed them in the pie, and when we got ready to eat it and cut it open, God it was full of beans. I'd reached the beans instead of the raisins. I passed out and fell back across the bed of the sheepwagon, and next day here was the dirty dishes and the bean pie.

CHAPTER SEVEN

SOME TALK ABOUT HORSES

A good cowboy ought to be able to get along with a horse. A horse fighter is not as good a hand as somebody that rides a horse that respects him, minds him, and does what he wants him to. I've seen guys go to working cattle, and the horse didn't turn just right, and they was beating and pounding on him because he wasn't doing right, and most of it was their own fault.

You can't fight a horse and work cows at the same time.

Horses can work under a horse fighter, but they work under fear. I know one man who's good about a lot of things. He can handle mean horses all right, and he rides some that a lot of people can't ride. The horses damn sure work for him, because if they don't, he will beat them to death. But it's not the best way. Other guys do the same kind of a job without being so rough.

It's a matter of temperament. Some guys know how to handle horses quiet and easy, and get them to do, and others, when they get mad, take it out on the horse.

I never have beat my horses. I try to make them mind. They all go to their stalls, and if one gets out of line, I'll snap him on the rear end, and he'll hurry in there, but he don't resent it. It's like a kid. They respect you, but you haven't abused them that much. They just know they'd better mind.

It's like giving orders to a bunch of men. Some bosses can give orders so the men respect every word they say

A communicative moment.

and others have to bawl men out so they're half mad. Some can say things and everybody laughs and feels good, but the others make everyone mad just by their tone of voice. The men do what they're told because they need the job, but they don't do it willingly. If they get a chance to cut a corner or do something a little dirty, they will. But if a man likes his boss, and if he can do a little something extra to help him out, he'll go ahead and do it. If he doesn't like his boss, he'll slide off.

There are hard-mouthed horses and soft-mouthed horses. There are "bars" up in a horse's mouth where the nerves are that feel the bit. When the bars get hurt and get dead, that makes a horse dead-mouthed. Some are made hard-mouthed by heavy hands on a bit, and their mouth just gets kind of numb. Anybody who always rides on a tight rein will make a hard-mouthed horse. A lot is in the horse, too, but you want to ride with a fairly easy bit, and give them slack and not get their jaws to cramping. I'm sure that a horse ridden with a tight rein must get his mouth aching from pressure against the bit. You train a horse the way you want him to work, and then somebody else starts riding him, and jerks him here and jerks him there. Even guys that are supposed to be good hands with horses can turn out to be horse killers instead.

You can tell horses like good treatment the way they come up to you. Today, I went over to the pasture and couldn't see a horse in sight, but I got to hollering around and pretty soon that little sorrel mare come trotting down out of the timber to get some oats, and here they all come. I took them into the corral and let them eat a few oats out of a pan. When I rode back this afternoon, the horses come off the hill down to see if there was a few more oats. If I didn't feed them any oats, they would stay up in the hills and pay no attention, but oats or any kind of grain makes horses come around and want to be fed.

After horses are broke to ride, my theory is that they enjoy people. When I'm feeding them, they'll come running to the barn. Or I can drive out with the pickup and feed one a few oats, and if I'm not in a big hurry they'll come on in to get some grain. If I didn't do that, I'd have to have a wrangling horse and go out after them.

A lot of people think a horse is just a dumb animal, but I wouldn't say any kind of animal is dumb. If somebody knows animals, they can get them to do what they want. There are people that can take pigs and train them. Sheep can seem dumb, but if you're a sheep man, and know how, you can get sheep to do what you want. They say "dumb animal," but animals are only dumb in some ways and up to a point. If you have studied the animal, you can do something with him. He can be trained.

Horses have to be trained. With tractors, if a man knows how to drive them, you get on and drive. Working with horses, you have to get a young horse in, get him harnessed up, and there is bound to be things that go wrong. You won't always have trouble, but one way or another some kind of mishap will often take place.

When people grew up with horses, even kids knew about them, just like today they know about cars. Any little guy would know enough to stay away from horses' feet, because they can kick you or step on you. Nowadays kids come out from town and don't have any fear of a horse. They will walk right into them. It's nothing against the kid. It's like me going to town; I don't know what the hell is going on!

Today, horses are a hobby. People think they can break a horse, and they don't know how, and they get him spoiled and have to sell him. They will buy a colt for their kids and think all they have to do is saddle up and ride him. But, they don't know how to train him. If he gets tangled up, they don't know what commands to give. It gets to where they can't ride him, and the colt don't know anything about going outside the corral. Pretty soon they have some trouble, or the colt throws somebody off, and they send him to the sale ring, and off he goes to the can because nobody will buy him. Nobody has the riding time to put in on a horse, or the time to work with one. People want a good gentle horse. They won't buy one that's been ridden just a few times, unless somebody has the use for him and thinks he's a good prospect.

When it comes to trading horses, there is a lot to know. There can be blemishes and things you can't see even in a good looking horse. You can't tell about disposition, or whether he will buck, or how good he is, but looks mean a lot.

It's practically the same thing as trading cars. You could get beat either way 'cause you can't tell from the looks of a car what the motor is like. It could be a fine looking body, but there might not be anything in it. Everybody wants to ride a good horse, but a good looking horse is not always a good one.

I knew one man who had a mare for sale that he said was gentle, so he sold her as a kid's pony or lady's horse. My neighbor here went over and put his saddle on her, and God, she went to bucking around the corral and bucked him off and the saddle, too. She was gentle to handle, but she had never been rode. They thought just because she was gentle, she was a kid's horse. That's what inexperienced people don't know—what a horse can do and how quick they can kill you. When you've handled horses all your life, and you see some inexperienced person getting on a horse that's supposed to be gentle, you know the horse could still get scared and hurt him. Gentle horses can be dangerous. I'd rather have a horse that was a little more snorty, that somebody had handled and trained.

There are lots of good horses wasted. I was at a sale in Sheridan recently where lots of horses just ran through the ring. It never was said if they were broke or not, but they probably had been monkeyed with and spoiled, so they went to the can. There are more horses today than when we were working horses, but nobody has any real use for them. It takes knowing how to break them. Of course, some of the horses in the sale ring are bought for other uses but the big end of them go right to the can.

Canner horse prices run up the price of saddle horses. If a thousand pound horse at fifty cents a pound for the can will bring $500, and they bring in a saddle horse and ride him through, why, you're going to have to beat the canner price to get him. So, if a horse has got any saddle prospects, he's going to bring $700 to $800. Horses is really high-priced now.

There is many horse lovers who are not horsemen. A horse lover will feed one, and take care of him, and maybe not do anything with him, but a horseman will ride him, and make him into something—a cow horse or a rope horse or whatever. A horse lover just pets him and doesn't do much with him. Training a horse takes a lot of hours. If you were paid at any regular wage for the number of hours it takes to make a horse you can do something with, you'd have a big price. When you pay a lot for a horse, you have to figure in the hours that have been put in on him.

If you take good care of a horse, and he's up in shape and hard, you can really set a ride on him. A horse that's fed good can stand a lot of riding. But if he is soft, then you should take it easier. I never rode many poor horses in my time. I always rode horses that was pretty hard, and I could set big rides on them and never worry. I took good care of them, so a hard day's ride didn't bother them. A horse is your friend if you take care of him and treat him right.

After you have rode a good many miles, you can tell from the feel of the horse under you if he is beginning to weaken, or whether he's still got plenty of go in him, or whether he is lazy. How many miles a horse can go, though, is sometimes a sixty-four dollar question. If a horse is on grass, but has been rode, he can still make an awful good ride. You could ride one thirty or forty miles a day. But, if he is soft, he can't go very far, because he is packing excess weight. So a horse on a good, stout grass can go a good ways, if he's been used all the time. A grain-fed horse is more stout and powerful if he's been used, but if he's just been fed grain and stood around, why he don't have much endurance either. He's got to be legged up. That means riding him and getting his legs under him so he's stout. So a grass-fed horse can go just as far, or further, than a grain-fed horse that hasn't been rode and legged up. It's just like a person; if you are walking out here, and you are used to walking, you'll go a lot further than somebody that has never walked very far.

When the sweat gets running down on both sides, you are generally using a horse pretty hard—unless it's awful hot. That happens quite a lot moving cattle; you've got sweat running down on both sides of your horse.

If I've got a horse that will walk and cover country fast, I'll make him walk. But if he can't walk very fast, I'll just hit a jog trot and keep jogging. Jogging probably bothers anybody that is young and tender, not as old and tough as me. I guess I'm so old and numb that I don't feel it. I rode in a lope a lot when I was young, and now I take a slower trend. But, a lot of times I will lope a ways, and then trot a ways, and walk a ways, and just kind of keep changing the horse off, depending on what kind of a horse I'm on and what has to be done.

Before tractors, everything on a ranch was done with horses. You worked in the fields, and hauled hay, and hauled all your supplies. If you had some old thing to haul right in your dooryard, you hooked up the team and wagon to haul it. Today, tractors do all the work. The only time a team is worked is if someone keeps them around to do some little job.

A lot of people have a team around, but they're really not broke to work any more. They are just drove a little bit. You hook them up for two months or so and get them going. Then, they're turned out until the next year. But, it's like with saddle horses. Work horses should be used all the time, otherwise they never get a chance to learn all the things they can do.

Nobody is really riding now. They ride a horse for two or three days, and he's big and fat, and then he's turned loose again. If he's got a little buck in him, or some ornery trick, and he pulls that and gets away with it, why he'll pull the same thing when you get him up again, and pretty soon he gets as so there ain't nobody can ride him.

If a horse is started, and kept going, and don't get away with any tricks, why then he gets gentler. But, if he's big and fat and comes in a-prancing, he hasn't learned anything. You've got to get that neck straightened out and get some of those wet saddle blankets drawed off of him. In the olden days, you'd take a bronc and get some rides in on him, and you wrangled the horses, and wrangled the cows. So you was using him some twice a day. You stayed right ahold of him. And you was doing lots of work over to the neighbors. You automatically had to use a horse.

Now everything's done by cars. If the mailbox is half a mile away, you use the car. And people load horses in trailers too much, and they don't have enough cow work to do. They might ride a horse and sweat him out for one day, and then he's turned loose for a week. Eventually, there won't be anybody riding much at all.

I never thought work horses were any smarter or dumber than saddle horses. Of course, a work horse is bigger and less active, but they're all about the same. Some horses are just smarter than others.

There are smart work teams that work and do things real good, and other horses that never did learn to do anything right. I've seen teams you could turn out of the barn, and if they was used to being hooked on a wagon, why they'd just pretty near walk up on each side of the wagon tongue by themselves.

You train horses to pull by starting with light loads, and then making the loads heavier, and trying to get them to go up easy against the weight. You keep giving them encouragement that they can pull, and after a while they just think they ain't stuck on anything. When they're colts, you start them with an old horse, and when you've got a good broke horse with a green horse, the old horse will start the load and the young horse picks up. After a while, he learns to start the same time as the old horse. So they get to working together.

What spoils a lot of horses is to get hooked onto a stuck load they can't possibly pull, and then for somebody to holler and scream at them, and hit them with the lines. They go up against that load, and they can't pull it, and they'll freeze up and won't go. After a horse has been balked once, he's liable to balk again, unless you are working him all the time. Then, you turn him loose for a while when he's "cold-shouldered." Cold-shouldered means a horse that won't pull, will just go up and hit and fly back. You call them cold-shouldered or "shotgun" horses.

My dad always said there wasn't balky horses; there was balky drivers. He was right, because if you don't whip and beat a team, they're not scared of you. They ain't afraid when they can't pull a load. The more excited and scared they get, the less they pull. They've got to be calm. Then, they will get down and pull all they can for you.

The same holds true for saddle horses. When you balk a saddle horse, he just don't want to go anywhere. They'll go for a little way, then turn around and go back to the barn. They can get barn sour. They just get to thinking they'll stay at the barn.

Those kinds of horses are dangerous. Bucking ain't so bad, but if you go to whipping on a balked horse when he can't have his own way, he'll go to raring and rare over backwards. That's what's dangerous. You've got to figure out some other way, 'cause you can only whip a horse so much. Maybe you can scare him, boo him, get him excited, and get him away from the buildings. There is no set pattern. Sometimes you can get a gunnysack or something, and get him scared of that, and he'll get to going and drifting.

With a balky horse you should take different rides—one day one way and another way the next, so he never figures out where you're going. It's repeating the same pattern that starts him to bulling you. He knows where's he's going, and that after about so long he's going back to the barn. If you get out on strange ground, he gets confused and doesn't know where he is, and then he'll start paying attention to you. There are many different ways, but you can't just whip on a balky horse because pretty soon he'll sull-balk, that is, go down on the ground. After a horse sulls, you can beat him to death. You've got to be careful of sulling a horse, keep figuring out something different. Anytime you can put a big ride on a horse out here on the hills and come back with a sweat, and the horse is tired, you don't have much trouble.

Work horses generally won't balk, if you don't whip and slash at them. You can tap them up a little bit to wake them up, but you never whip and beat them. Then, when you get them on a stuck load, they don't get scared. If they can't pull it, you can unload some and they will try again.

If you take a team and hook them on too heavy a load when they don't know how to pull, and their shoulders are soft, and you go to screaming at them, one horse will lunge, and then the other one, and they can't pull, and pretty soon they give up. They won't even tighten up the tugs. That's the part of the harness that attaches to the doubletrees. Generally, one horse will throw his head over the other horse's hame, and then you know you've had it. You can get them started on a buggy and in the fields, and maybe they will pull a fair load as long as it's rolling, but when you need to really get down and pull, they will quit you. They've learned that.

You can work a team with open bridles, if they're broke that way, but generally people use blinders because they claim a horse works better. If a lazy horse had an open bridle, and you got ready to hit him, he could see you, and he would jump up ahead and fall back. With blinders he wouldn't see you when you tapped him up with a whip. He'd stay up a little better. Also, when a horse can't see what's dragging behind him, he don't get scared as much.

Then there is such a thing as a stay chain. The doubletree comes across, and the horses are one on each side of the tongue, and the chain goes over and back to the load. It makes it so that when both horses is even they are pulling, but if one horse goes out and hits, it don't jerk the other horse back. It will start the load and the other horse picks up.

A team has got to really get down and pull hard on a load, keep getting scratched down lower to the ground, and keep a-hanging, and pretty soon the load will come loose. But, it takes a team that will hang that way. A team that goes up and hits something might jar it and start it if it's not too heavy, but they won't stay there and pull.

I have seen pictures of these pulling contests where horses is pulling high and going fast, but to me a pulling horse has got to have his head down and be humped up, and have his feet under him putting power on. To me, a team would start bigger loads if they would just get down and keep laying into it and scratching. I have seen horses pull that was putting so much power on their legs they looked like their bellies was down on the ground.

I don't think teams will ever come back. There will always be some kind of gas and machinery. Horses are obsolete because people are used to getting things done with gasoline. And where would you find people to work horses? If you had a ranch today and wanted to do all your haying like they used to, even if you had the good broke horses, it would be hard to find anybody that would know how to drive them. There is a lot to knowing how to work even a good team. It's a lost art.

When tractors began to come in around 1928 or so, they turned a lot of horses out to pasture. Horses was cheap, and there was lots of land, and people would kick horses out and not pay much attention. Some was cripples or had something wrong with them, so they let them go. They never kept the studs castrated, and the horses got inbred. Some had great big heads and little bitty bodies. Then, guys went through and cleaned up the range of these horses. If they were not claimed, they would be sold to canneries. I never was in on any of that, but I've seen them run these horses in when they was cleaning up this BLM [Bureau of Land Management] land. They'd run in five, or six, or a dozen unbroke horses, and you would buy them like bananas—by the bunch. But horses was cheap. Man, if you had the horses today that they cleaned off them ranges!

I've rode many a horse for five dollars. They weren't the best, but they would put you ahorseback.

In the early days, when they first started to improve range horses, work horses were used, and a lot of people raised and sold good big studs. People took pride in raising good work horses. Back then horses were crossed up with any type of horses. They was mixed breed horses, what they called "cold-blooded," bred up from Indian ponies. Belgian and Percheron horses were plentiful in the country at that time, and when they was bred to small mares, some of the offspring would get pretty thick and heavy. But, they never got too big, and people rode them and worked them.

About that time, the government came in with good thoroughbred studs and began breeding saddle horses. They called them "Remount" studs because they were used for breeding up the cavalry. They were crossed on the Indian mares and smaller-type work mares. These Indian ponies were a pretty good kind of cow horse. That's what the old timers rode. They wasn't too big, but they was tough.

I think it was probably along 1927 or 1928 that I first heard of a government stud, but they may have been around earlier than that. We was far out, and you didn't go places and see things like you do today.

I know by 1936 there were lots of government horses. A lot of people tried to sell horses to the Remount Program, because if a horse passed inspection he would bring $160 for use in the Army. Then, not long after World War II, the quarter horses started coming in. For a long time, the quarter horse was the popular horse, and you didn't hear anything about thoroughbred crosses and stuff. They started out with the little old chunky bull-type of quarter horses that reminded me of Percheron or Belgian colts, and they kept breeding them up until now a quarter horse looks more like a thoroughbred.

Buckskin Joe was the first quarter horse stud in the country that I heard of. He went pretty strong from about 1947 to 1950. He belonged to Morris and Teunis Clark on the Bar V, and he had a big name in the country. This Morris Clark was a wealthy boy from the east who started these quarter horses. He had men breaking them, and everybody wanted a Buckskin Joe colt. I never did see the horse, but I've seen pictures of him, and there is a picture in the Elks Club of a bunch of colts that's supposed to have been by Buckskin Joe.

Quarter horses became really popular. Calf roping started, and they wanted a horse that was fast just for a little ways—over a quarter mile or so. You could rope a calf off them, because they could make a fast run, but they are not long-running horses. The rodeo hands started using them, and they still want a horse to perform like that, but the rope horses are bigger now.

A quarter horse comes from a thoroughbred cross. They picked the shorter-type, more compact horses with heavier loin and muscle. They don't have the endurance that a thoroughbred does. Of course, quarter horse guys can still start an argument, but the government always kept to thoroughbred horses for the cavalry. For ranch horses, my preference would be a thoroughbred and quarter horse cross. It puts a little go to them, and slows them down a little, too.

Thoroughbreds have a lot of fire to them. They've got legs under them, and they can travel, and they've got a lot of endurance. I like a thoroughbred when he is started right and he gets confidence. He will work for you just as good as a quarter horse, but you've got to be quiet with him and not abuse him. They're horses you can't change riders on. There's been a lot of thoroughbred horses spoiled on big outfits, because they're hot and fiery, and somebody fights them, and they get to fighting back and bucking. They're smart. If you get them broke right, they're the gentlest horse there is, but if you get them started wrong, they can be the meanest.

On a big range, studs pick their bunch of mares and fight off all the other studs. They run in their own territory, and if any other stud comes in there, there's a big fight. Of course, there's bachelor studs that run through the country. They always get whipped out, so they're never with a bunch of mares. I read one time how they run by themselves, and some guy walking through a country claimed that studs whipped out that way were dangerous. He thought they would even attack a man.

A mare will sometimes take a colt away from another mare, when she has lost her own. One time this big old work mare had lost a colt. I seen it dead. And there was an old stray mare with a colt in there with them. After a while someone said to me, "God, was you wrong! That old work mare has got a colt sucking." Well, I knew it was dead, and we come to find out this poor old stray didn't have a colt any more. The work mare had got the colt away from her.

An old dry mare sometimes will try to granny a colt—take it away from its mother. And I've heard them say that when two mares with colts run together, one of them will sometimes try to take both colts.

It's nicer to have geldings around than mares. If horses are used to running together, it's all right to have both, but more horses get crippled with mares around, because there's always herders in the bunch. They get to fighting. When there is a whole bunch of geldings running together, and you throw in a strange mare, you're going to get a horse crippled. They are like men and their lady friends. So, it's better just to have a straight bunch of geldings.

Then there's mules. To get a pretty saddle mule, they breed good thoroughbred or other saddle mares to jackasses. Mules don't reproduce. It takes a jack donkey and a mare to produce a mule. A female mule is a jenny, and a male is just a mule. You have to castrate them, because they would behave like a stud even though they can't reproduce.

A stallion bred to a female donkey produces a hinny. I have just seen one or two hinnies. Hinny mules will sell for pretty good prices in Colorado and places. They even have clubs where people ride and rope off hinnies, and do cutting work with them. I used to ride an old work mule, Molly, in harness, but otherwise I have never rode a mule. They claim they are surefooted and nice to ride, with a good walk.

They used to buck mules in rodeos. They jump fast and wicked, but they don't hit the ground as hard as a horse. But, they don't use mules too much in rodeo bucking strings, only in little old farmer rodeos.

Most generally, a good cutting horse is not a good rope horse. A cutting horse is trained to keep his head right on a cow. A rope horse is supposed to get right up on the cow—I'm talking about in an arena—so you can throw a rope on easy. But, the kind of cowboy I was, I never was too good at any of it.

You can rope some and work cattle some off most horses the average rancher rides. Even if you are riding a green bronc, you can do something on him, up to a point. The old cow horses kind of do everything, even if maybe they're not the best. The big end of horses I ride are really not cutting horses, or rope horses, or anything special.

For a horse to get cow sense, it takes a couple of years of riding nowadays. I figure it takes a year of steady use to make a horse foolproof, so you can do anything you want to do on him. I don't know where cow sense in a horse comes from. Whether it's thoroughbreds, quarter horses, or cold bloods, some horses are smart and just like to dodge a cow. If the sire or mother had good cow sense, as they call it, your chances of getting a smart colt can be pretty good. But, other times I've seen a colt out of a mare that was a really good cow horse, and the colt was a dummy.

They've got to have brains to want to do it, but they've also got to be trained and take to it. It's the same thing as a person. One guy takes to be a mechanic and the next guy to be a cowpuncher. Everybody has a line, and I think horses run the same way.

Any kind of a cow horse needs plenty of riding, and turning, and keeping cows in front of them. If they have cow sense, they'll start learning when you want the cow turned. To start a horse, you pull him one way and another, trying to get him to work a cow, tapping him with reins, or touching him with a spur a little bit, so he answers to your response. Once they get to working, they get interested and wanting to know. They get to the right place at the right time if they can.

When they know you're taking out a cow, and she starts to turn back, they'll try to head her off. As soon as you single out one cow, she'll split off, and then the horse will start watching her. He'll keep his eyes right on her. From day after day following cows, they learn that when a cow turns, and you kind of cue them a little, they're supposed to go back. They're watching the cow, which they have to do to be a good cow horse.

If a cow breaks back, and you are riding a green horse, you should turn that horse back easy, because a green horse can't turn fast enough. A green horse can get to running by the cattle, and that's a hard habit to break. He just doesn't see them. You want to start turning him with slow stuff, so he gets to following them and picks up the idea. A green horse is not coordinated to turn. He's going too fast, and he goes on by, and he don't know which way the cows went. They will get to doing that 'til you can't hardly teach them to turn back.

A lot of horses won't rein at all, but, if they are following the cow when she turns, they will turn back with her. If you went out here and tried to turn a cow horse around with nothing in front of him, you couldn't turn him on an acre of ground, but he will follow a cow. I was no reining man, but most of the horses that I have rode in my time learned what to do.

If I get in an arena and start trying to rope, or make the horse change leads, I don't do it right. I'm kind of like a horse; I've got to have a cow in front of me. If a cow's going to the left, I automatically put pressure on to bring the horse to the left. But when you don't have anything in front of you, you forget what you are doing. Or anyway, I do.

A good reining horse will not be a good cow horse, because if a horse is reined real good, and you give him the cue, he is not watching cows. He is watching you, the rider. And when you pull up on a reining horse to stop him, he is trained to back up a lot. A cow horse will back up some, but he's watching the cow.

On a reining horse, a lot is done with the hands, but a good reining man also does a lot with his legs. He puts leg pressure from one side to the other. If you put pressure on the right side, the horse will go to the left, and the same the other way. So there is a lot to training and riding a reining horse.

I never rode many bucking horses, but from riding horses in the hills, I can tell you that if you have your reins about right, and a horse jumps and throws his head down and you fall back on him, maybe you'll pull him up the first jump. If he's got the slack, he'll go on and buck.

There's a lot of different ways you can tell when a horse is going to buck. If he's tight and humped up when you saddle him, and that old saddle is setting kind of high on end, he could buck with you. And when you get on him, you can feel the way his muscles are—if he's tight, he ain't traveling free. When he loosens up, and you can feel the saddle loosen up, you figure you're on the road. Of course, a horse can get scared, and you don't have no warning. He just blows up and bucks. But, after you have rode a lot of horses, you can tell just going around the corral whether a horse is loose or tight. It's something you have the feel of in your butt.

A good bucking horse for rodeo use has to be tough, and hard-headed, and want to buck. You can't pull him up. He will buck regardless. If he really wants to buck, you can pull so much on a horse's head, but he will get high enough in the air, and fall back, and get his head or take it sideways, and jerk you loose. He gets mad and throws his whole heart at it. Other horses that's nervous, or more kind, give up bucking.

It takes a tougher horse to be a bucking horse than it does to be a cow horse. A lot of bucking horses is made due to some accident. Often, it's because a horse gets spoiled. Say he gets scared and bucks somebody off. Once he finds out he can succeed, he'll go on from there. If a horse never bucks anybody off, he may know how to buck, but he don't think about it or do it. But, after a horse has throwed somebody off, he has a tendency to try it again.

In order to produce a bucking horse, the first thing would be to find a stud that had an ornery disposition, and wanted to buck himself. Today, thoroughbred studs are bred to be quieter, but it used to be that they had a hot disposition. Crossing them on a Belgian or a Percheron mare could get you a big, active horse that weighed between 1,400 and 1,500 pounds. That cross made a lot of good saddle broncs. Size is important, because they want big saddle broncs that hit the ground hard. A little horse under a saddle is more wiry and fast, and the bareback horses are more like that. They are rode different and they throw more action.

Bucking horses are all flanked with a strap covered with sheepskin pulled tight around their flanks. A horse naturally hates anything around his flanks, so they can actually be trained to be bucking horses, because that flank strap will make them buck. A lot of horses wouldn't buck if they weren't flanked. One horse I rode for five years used to stumble and fall down. He was a gentle horse, but he was sold into a bucking string. He wouldn't have bucked ordinarily, but after he'd been bucked a time or two, he kind of liked it. As far as I know, he is still bucking.

All bronc riders today are supposed to spur the horse out of the chute—spur clear back and throw their legs pretty near to the cantle of the saddle. They make that rhythm so when a horse comes out bucking flanked, he don't spin and dodge like the old horses. They call them "trashy" bucking horses. They go more straight and kick high, so when the horses go down in front, these boys have got the spurs in their shoulders. When the horses kick up, that brings the riders up, and they spur behind, keeping rhythm with the horse.

Unlike the average cowboy, rodeo contestants are trained riders, but it's hard for them to ride a horse that spins. They are used to riding one pattern. Ducking and diving horses are harder to ride; you've got to figure out which way they're going. Today, when you see a horse that comes out of the chute turning and whirling, he usually bucks somebody off pretty easy. The old-time cowboys was used to riding horses that turned and dodged. They rode with a deeper saddle and with more swells. They wasn't contesting. They was staying on top to get some work done.

I never was a bronc rider. I had to ride what the women rode! But, over the years I never had much trouble with horses bucking. I have rode horses that bucked with other guys, and I got plumb away with them and got them to going. I've used horses you had to know how to get on, and that you had to fool around to get off. You might call that "stealing a ride." I managed to foul them one way or another, walking them around in the corral, or jerking them around, or keeping them into a fence. They wasn't kids' horses, but, after I got them warmed up, they wasn't bucking horses either. I could usually figure out a horse, and get along with him, and get his confidence. I've rode horses that I knew could buck me off, and there were maybe one or two along the line that I couldn't ride and somebody else rode. I never handled no really tough bucking horses. I'd let somebody else handle them. I never was no wild cowboy.

But, there is something funny about the horse business. Everybody laughs if a guy gets bucked off. A man can get hurt, but they still laugh. It was all danger, but God they would laugh. And if a greenhorn acted smart with a bunch of guys, they would damn sure figure out a way to get him bucked off. They was rougher on young fellers in bygone times than they are now.

Broncs is the same as women; you've got to keep them confused. If you're riding a horse out here, and you keep going different ways and keep his mind on something else beside looking back and seeing you, you can get along. That's just an expression I use about women. I can't explain it. I've got a lot of crazy ideas, and my dictionary would be hard to put together.

If you think about it, horses have a sad life. One guy will ride a horse and make him mind, but making him mind is one thing and abusing him is something different. You can be kind to a horse and handle him, and whip him around a little, and he'll like you. But, being mean is a different thing. My horses would always mind me, but I never abused them.

My dad used to say it was nice when they started using cars to go to dances. They used to tie saddle horses to a post in the cold, and not even feed them for a day or two. Horses were worked on short feed and starved. Guys would ride them clear into the ground to get the work done. Now, they can abuse their car if it won't start, and all it costs them is money. A poor horse wouldn't have any way to fight back. He had to take whatever was done to him. Today, if they wreck an automobile, it costs the man, but there is no pain. You can abuse a tractor and not take care of it or service it, but it has no feelings. A poor horse's body was there, and if he didn't get nothing to eat, he suffered. So, that's the difference.

It is sad when you lose your faithful horses. If you're not around them so long it makes it easier—like one summer I worked teams that I never saw again. You don't get as close to them as to a horse you have for several years. Old Amigo here probably means more to me than any of the others, because he's been here twelve years like I have. People say, "Well, I wouldn't want to send a horse to a canner," but it's sometimes more humane to send him to a canner than to let him run in the pasture.

I know a guy who pensioned a horse he had when he was a young feller, and he kind of forgot about him. He found the horse dead in the hills. He didn't get around to shoot him in time. He said he really felt bad, because it was an old faithful horse. He had several good years a-running, but after a while time ran out. I think it's fine if anybody pensions a horse, and he runs out to pasture and stays in good shape. But, when it comes the day that his teeth go bad so he can't get any feed, and he gets poor, and he starves to death by inches, then the can is a better place.

CHAPTER EIGHT

EARLY JOBS AND MARRIAGE (1937–1941)

In 1937 I worked at the 3T Ranch in the hay crew. My mother's half-brother, Cap Storm, was the manager there. I and a fellow called Lyle Storm took my old '28 Chevy Coupe and drove up to see if we could get a job. They had somewhere around 5,000 cattle running out in the hills and more riders than Carter's got pills, but I never was around any cattle that summer, because we didn't get there 'til about the tenth of June. Branding was pretty well over and we went right to haying.

The place had been bought the fall before by the King family. They was wealthy oil people from Ohio. Young Bob King was only twenty-one, and his dad wanted him to have some responsibility, so he got hold of the ranch and got him going. With his dad behind him, he'd borrowed money through the Bank of Commerce. Cap Storm was field man for the bank—the guy that goes around counting cattle and looking after the bank's interests—and he seen that they'd have to do something with that outfit, because it was in awful shape. The bank contacted King senior, and he asked them to recommend someone to manage the place. That's how my uncle got to be there. The 3T was a wonderful place with 1,000 acres of irrigated ground—and hay everywhere. They had a lot of outside pasture, but like most places, they ran too many cattle. That year, they were doing a lot of building and fixing up the water works, because they needed good drinking water. With the construction and hay crews, there were fifty men on payroll, with thirty-five of them at the main ranch.

I worked for $40 a month and board, and, by God, it was good board. They had a commissary for the main ranch and two other ranches, and Mrs. King bought the best. She'd look over the canned goods, and if something wasn't her brand, she made them take it back. They butchered a beef every week. At the cookhouse, they had a chore man that milked the cows, took care of the pigs, and brought the meat in. One woman was the head cook, and there was a second cook, and a boy washing dishes, and the chore man helped with the odd jobs. There was a great big icehouse with ice over the top and on the sides, and that's where they'd hang the beef they'd kill every week. It would come out in chunks to the camps—just what you could cut up and use real quick.

There was a great big, long, old bunkhouse with maybe four rooms in it and enough places for all thirty-five men. There was a washroom where you went in and washed, and you had to pack the water in for that. For the shower in the summer time, they piped water half a mile from a reservoir, and if you could get there first, the water would be warm in the pipes, but when it started draining out of reservoir, it was real cold. So everybody would try to get the first Saturday night shower.

The bunkhouse had a room with some chairs in it—what you'd call a living room—and a card table. We used to play nickel-a-hand rummy, and that was our pastime of evenings. It was a log bunkhouse with a tin roof, I believe, and it was very cool. There was big rooms, and clothes closets, but nothing was locked up. There might be a lot of guys putting their clothes in the same closet, and if somebody quit, he could just take somebody else's coat or something. Most of the guys had a little old suitcase stuck under the bed with stuff in it, and everybody had their own bedroll. At that time, if you didn't have a bedroll, they wouldn't hire you.

There was lots of good times around bunkhouses. If somebody was a musician, he would play and sing. And of course, you had to be pretty good-natured, and be one of the boys around the bunkhouse, or they would run you out, because there was always lots of pranks. If you wanted to be a loner, and get mad at everybody, you'd be mad every day, because they'd make it so tough on you that you might as well leave. They'd pull pranks on the outside and the inside and everything else just to hear you bitch—from tying your overshoes together, to putting stuff in your bed, or anything else that would cause a little disturbance—and you couldn't whip the whole crowd.

Nobody had much in the way of dress clothes. This lady up above the outfit done quite a pile of laundry for a quarter. She done it all on an old hand-scrub board, and she picked up a lot of dollars from the men. The only clothes I had with me to go to a dance with was a new pair of overalls and a white shirt or two.

Some of the time we'd go to Kaycee. There was a dance hall at Kaycee, but some old people lived up there in the school house, and they would have dances, too—every two weeks. Everybody put in a little money and a quarter for a dance ticket, and the old lady and him would have a big midnight supper. Somebody would play the violin, and the dances would last until daylight. There was always lots of men, but not many girls. I have seen a dance quadrille where they would put an apron on somebody, and he was supposed to be the woman. I have done that, and it's kind of hard to change sides to go around the other way.

At that time, everybody was drinking beer at the dances, and they thought they was having a big time. Times is changed. Now, if you drink beer it makes you dead. I guess there is still some that drink it, but I can't drink beer when I go to dances. I just go to sleep.

For some of June and all through the month of August, I had a lot of fun at the 3T bunkhouse. At 5:00 A.M., they'd ring a bell for the horse wrangler, and another bell at 5:30 to tell everybody to get the harness on their teams. It was the chore man's job to jingle the bells, and there was four bells of a morning. At 5:45 everybody was supposed to be out of bed, and then there was a bell at 6:00 for breakfast, and you'd better be at the breakfast table at 6:00. You had to keep track of the bells, or you'd wonder where you was at.

Most of the time, I was up at the Willow Creek haying camp that was only about a mile from the school house that we danced in. Several times, I didn't get home until daylight. One time it was my turn to wrangle the horses, and I got them in, harnessed my team, ate breakfast, got on one of them old buckrakes, went to bucking in hay, and never did get a wink of sleep.

The bunkhouse up at the haying camp had nothing modern about it at all. It didn't have any windows or electricity, and we had to pack water from a well. All we had was an old coal-oil lamp. We quit work at 5:30, and the meal was on the table at 6:00, and we'd turn out our horses and maybe throw a few horseshoes, and then set around and play cards for a little. We had to build a sagebrush fire to keep the mosquitos out, and most generally we went to bed when it got dark. I used to wash my work clothes in Willow Creek in the cold water—just rinse out my work shirt and overalls and throw them on a bush to dry. Like a tramp.

I did the wrangling for three of the older guys that didn't like to ride. They got up early, and they'd always have a saddle horse right at the bunkhouse door for me. When I'd come out, I'd step on the old horse and wrangle. I done that for a goodwill turn, because they didn't like to ride, and they was nice guys, and I was young, so I could go whip the horses in.

I had a big team of dappled gray Percheron mares. Their names was Kit and Gray. On a big outfit like the 3T, you very seldom know the names of the horses, so I named them myself. They issued harness there, and I had an old set, but there was a kid driving a rake who didn't care much what his gear looked like. You could tell, because he had new harness and it wasn't adjusted up. One day I offered him a quarter to trade harness. So he took the quarter, and I took the new harness and put it on this dappled gray team. They was really pretty, and I used them all through the haying.

My team was a good buckrake team. For that, it takes a horse that will back up good. They have to walk up on the stacker and then back off. This team would come up and back right off, and they was lively. They had good mouths on them, so you could pull up on one and stop her, and the other would step ahead and go to spin the buckrake around.

At that time, they used an overshot stacker with arms that laid on the ground with teeth on them. You came up with this bull rake, or buckrake, with a horse hooked on each side, and bucked the hay up onto the head of the stacker. The horses would back off, and then another team would pull, and these arms went up in the air and dropped the load on the haystack.

A rake was very dangerous. If you fell off the front of it, you could be dragged to death. The rake would keep dragging, and there was no way to get out from under it, unless you hit a ditch. Your only chance of getting out would be to hit some low ground, so the rake let you roll out. I knew a man who lost his boy raking hay. He was a little too young to be on a rake, and he slipped and fell some way, and the team run off and dragged him to death.

When I got there the first of June, I was booked as a mowing machine man. Nobody knew anything about the horses. Some of them wasn't broke to work very good. My first team was a pair of spoiled, big blacks, and I started hooking them up the first morning figuring I'd drive them to the mower. One reared up in the harness, and fell back, and tangled up the lines, and they started to run with one tug hooked. They got away from me and pretty near knocked down the yard fence around the Kings's big house. From there, they ran into a round corral, so I shut the gate on them and got them untangled. Then I got another team that would work. Before the day was over, they had seven runaways. The horses were green, and the men didn't know them. At first, it was a pretty wild outfit, but after they got things lined out and got some work in on them, the horses went to haying.

All I did at the 3T was haying that one summer. Cap Storm got let out the first of September. He didn't get along with young Bob King, who wanted to spend money, but my uncle wouldn't okay it. So the Kings brought in a new manager, an oil man from Ohio, and a lot of fellows quit. They said they wasn't going to work for that kind of guy, and I left the first of September, too.

I went back down home for the winter, and went to work at a small sawmill owned by George Redding. They was getting out ties, and I used a team to skid logs into the mill to be sawed up. They was cut pretty close around the mill, and I would pull them in, a log or two at a time, with a chain or skidding tongs that are like ice tongs that you hook into the logs. So I skidded logs there for awhile, until a storm at Thanksgiving shut the mill down. After that I helped the folks cut some wood and just pondered around for the rest of the winter.

About the first of June, I took off from Hulett in an old '28 Chevy and drove to Sheridan. I was with another boy that was about fifteen years old. The roads were oiled, but nothing like they are nowadays, and it took us eight hours, because the Chevy wouldn't go but thirty or thirty-five miles an hour. We ate supper in town, where we didn't know anybody, and drove out to Downer Addition on Soldier Creek. This boy's folks had a small house with a vacant lot right close, so I rolled my bed out on the grass that night. The next day, I went out to the Fryberger ranch where Harry Allen was foreman. I knew him from haying at the 3T the summer before.

Mrs. Harry Allen was the head cook, and six to eight hands were working there. I visited all day, and stayed overnight. "I sure am sorry I haven't got a place to put you," Allen told me, "but I'm filled up on men."

I slept in a log building that they used for a granary—put a bed in there on the cement floor—and it was a nice cool place. The next morning, I'd already bid them goodbye and was rolling up my bed, when I heard Allen coming click-clack, click-clack, across the cement. He was a fast-stepping little guy. "Don't roll up your bed," he said, "two guys just quit." That's how I come to work there. It was a good place to work: They had good grub, and we got $40 a month.

Fryberger's was a sheep outfit. I worked in the hayfields putting up about 400 tons of hay with horses the first summer. They had sheep on the Big Horn and Wolf mountains. The sheep came off the Big Horns the first of September, and the lambs was cut off and herded for a while on green meadows, and then put into the feed lot, and fattened out, and shipped to Omaha. The Wolf Mountain sheep came in a little later, and the same was done with them.

That was my first time helping feed sheep. They was in pens with hayracks to eat out of, and every night and morning we'd spread whole oats and barley in troughs. You'd open up the gate, and let a bunch of sheep go in and eat their grain, and when they was done, you'd turn them out and let in some others. We had between 1,500 and 1,600 lambs on feed as near as I can remember. My part was to haul hay and grain and throw off straw—just general ranch work. There was a chore man, too, who generally milked five or six cows, and Fryberger grew up the dairy calves for beef for the ranch.

There were twenty work horses on the outfit, and everything was done with them. The second summer I was there, they got a McCormick-Deering Farm-All tractor with a mowing machine. The tractor mowed the hay down, but they still raked and bucked it in with horses.

That fall was the first time I ever plowed with six horses. I was working a two-way plow, plowing sod. The ground was irrigated, but it was hard plowing. Even with three horses abreast and three in the lead I only turned one 16-inch furrow, so I didn't cover very many acres. On old ground it was easier, because it turns easier. With those six horses and a gang plow that turned two furrows, I could plow five or six acres a day.

I used to get up at five a.m. and have my six head of horses harnessed before breakfast at six. When I was in practice, I could harness six head of horses in thirty minutes and groom them, too. You had to know which collar went on which horse, because collars run in all sizes, and I'd hang the harness according to which side each horse worked on. I used to pride myself that I could have my horses harnessed and be in the bunkhouse waiting for breakfast ahead of everybody else.

Some funny things happened at Fryberger's that year. Harry Allen gets up early one morning, and in the dimness of the coal-oil lights he goes to the medicine cabinet and takes out a bottle he thought was the medicine he was taking, but he takes a spoonful of iodine instead. Of course it burned, and he spit all over to get it out of his mouth. When we came to breakfast, he was sitting looking kind of sick, and he said, "God, I pretty near poisoned myself this morning." And his brother, Everett, said, "Any damned fool that would get up before daylight *ought* to poison himself!"

Another time, we were late getting the chores done after dark, and a hand named Edward throwed a bucket into the grain room where there wasn't any light. Harry's voice hollered out of there, "What in the hell is going on? You hit me on the head with that bucket!" It turned out he'd just come in from sheep camp on his saddle horse. Edward shouted back: "If you got your chores done in daylight, you wouldn't *be* hit in the head with a bucket!"

I slept in the granary at Fryberger's for two or three weeks. Then a guy moved out, and I got a good room—or so I thought. I goes in there, and holy Christ, there's bedbugs crawling all over. So one Sunday when everybody was gone, I and another feller cleaned up the main part of it. One old guy who slept back there was laughing at us. He'd gone to town and got himself some sulfur and throwed it over his mattress, and that kept them out of his clothes. Some bunkhouses were very bad that way. They would be full of bedbugs, and you didn't have anything to kill them with. So, when they got to eating on you too bad, why you'd put kerosene on the springs, and pour some kerosene on the mattress.

Another old guy in the Fryberger bunkhouse was a little off in the upper storey. Instead of putting chunk coal in the bunkhouse stove, he'd go get some of that slack, fine-powdered coal, because he thought he was saving the outfit money. Well, if you throw slack in a heating stove, it will set about so long, and keep getting hotter, and then it will explode. It'll even blow the lids up on cookstoves, and they don't have a heavy draft, but in a heating stove with a good draft, it will blow up worse.

So this guy was sitting in front of this stove with the draft wide open, cutting his toenails with one foot on the floor and the other one up on his knee, when the stove exploded and throwed hot coals on his feet. He danced a jig all over the floor, and he cussed and stormed! I was sitting there with Everett, Harry's brother, and he said, "God damn it, burn them big chunks! They was still running out of the chute when we got that last load, and the outfit can afford some more coal!"

Harry's son, Howard, worked on the railroad, but he come back to work on the ranch that winter. He went into town one Saturday night to get a haircut and got to drinking beer until the bars closed. Finally, at the Mission Bar, they was hollering, "Drink up! We're closing!" It was snowing like the devil, and Howard was so drunk he couldn't drive, so I took off in the snowstorm and drove us home about three in the morning.

I knew I couldn't get Howard upstairs to where he usually slept, so I drove him to the bunkhouse, and got the chore man to help me pack him in. We throwed him on the springs of a bed without a mattress. By six or so it was still storming, but Howard and I was supposed to feed these sheep, so we goes to the barn to harness our horses. "Christ," Howard says, "the least you fellers could have done was to throw me on a mattress! I got coil-spring marks all over my side!" So we goes up to breakfast, and Howard takes one look at the cup of coffee, and he leaves, sick, and I'm right behind him. We went out and tried to haul hay, but the wind was a-blowing, and we couldn't haul no hay. Howard's folks was mad. His dad, being boss, said, "You guys aren't going to town anymore!" He put me on the night shift and Howard on in the daytime.

Sometimes we went to dances at the Big Goose Community Hall where they had a three or four-piece orchestra, including a piano and a saxaphone. Whiskey was legal then, but nobody mixed drinks. You'd go outside and take a drink out of a bottle with no chaser or nothing. A few of the young girls used to drink some of that whiskey, but none of the older women.

Howard and I used to get a fifth of whiskey and pour a pint of straight alcohol into it. That alcohol was 100 per cent, and it threw a jolt into that old Hermitage or Sunnybrook. Guys would drink that, and pretty soon they'd wonder what we was drinking. They couldn't stand much of it. We thought it was fun to get these guys loop-legged on our whiskey. It would take your breath away and blow your head off.

I only herded sheep for three days at Fryberger's. They took some groceries out to the regular herder one snowy morning, and he stepped to the door and said, "See them sheep? You take them!" So Harry tells me to take over, and Everett brought my bed and some grub out and said, "See you in the spring." I didn't know if I was going to lose the damned sheep or what. I didn't know anything about throwing them back to the bed ground, or how to let them spread out, or anything like that. I was there two nights, and then they brought out this other herder, and I was glad to see him! I wouldn't want to do that steady. If you are really out herding sheep, you can't get off Saturday night or no time.

It used to be a penitentiary offense to walk off and leave a bunch of sheep without notifying the owner. At Fryberger's one time, a guy left the sheep to go check on his wife in town—to see how many boyfriends she had—and there comes a blizzard and he couldn't get back. So along in the middle of the night, Fryberger's gets a call from a voice they didn't recognize that says, "Your sheep is alone and will be alone tomorrow night." They went to check on the sheep, and they were all there, and they got another herder real quick. The other guy was scared they'd have him arrested, but they just paid his wages and let him go.

They used to take herders out and leave them a week or more at a time. Nowadays, you are supposed to see a sheepherder every other day to see he's all right, and you're considered at fault if you don't check on him.

Fryberger's was where I met Pauline. She come to work there the first summer, and we had a lot of fun visiting around the cookhouse where she was Mrs. Harry Allen's helper. We never went out on a date 'til later. She was there from August to October, when she got laid off and went to nurse's school in Rapid City. But the school closed the next spring, and Fryberger's hired her back in March, about the time we were lambing and there was more of a crew. If Pauline had stayed down in nurse's training, she'd wouldn't have had me on her apron strings.

I'd go up to visit her, but we wouldn't want to be caught in the house alone, so when we saw a car coming in, we'd blow out the light, and I'd go to the bunkhouse and Pauline would go upstairs. One time Harry came home and grabbed hold of the lamp chimney, and it was still hot. He was cussing and storming about burning himself, and it was a giveaway that Pauline and I had been sitting up.

About May, we got started going out to dances, and that was all we ever went to except maybe a show. And we did go to the rodeo together that year. In the fall, we started going steady, and in January of '40 we was married—on January 18, my mother's birthday. There was no place to live at Fryberger's, so we moved to Meade Creek, twelve miles southeast of Sheridan where Pauline's Aunt, Mabel Hublitz, had a place. Her husband had died with a heart attack, and she'd sold off all her cattle and horses, but she still had some land to farm, so we went down there April first and farmed on a shoestring.

It was a sharecrop deal. There was about 100 acres of hay ground, and I put in twenty-five or thirty acres of wheat and a little barley. I had to irrigate, and put up the hay, and Pauline's Aunt Mabel got half the hay and half the grain. I had never run irrigating water before, but I covered those 100 acres, working from daylight to dark. I've still got the scars on my feet from that irrigating:

Pauline's dad gave me an old pair of rubber boots, because we didn't have no money, and they leaked, and didn't fit me right, and my heels all blistered and peeled up. You can do that kind of thing when you're young and think you are going to get ahead.

The first cutting we got alfalfa seed, and today, at a dollar a pound, it would have made a lot of money. It sold then for ten cents a pound. My total share out of it was $600, which today wouldn't be very much, but $600 was more than I'd have made working somewhere. With some grocery bills and stuff to pay, I had a little money left over.

A guy named Todd lived above us there. He had an old team that would get up against the gate and rub on it until they got the loop off, and then come down the road and get into the alfalfa fields. We'd run them out, and they'd saunter back home. Well, one night they goes down to Ralph Willey's place, half a mile below where we was, and rubbed the gate down, and they and Willey's dairy cows got in on the alfalfa.

The next morning, the hired hands seen that team with the cows out in the alfalfa field again, so they took two washtubs and tied them onto the horses tails, so the tubs just hit the ground. It was an ornery trick, because it scares the living hell out of a horse to have something drag off him that way. Their idea was that if the team ran right by Todd's place, he'd take better care of them.

So, early in the morning when I was going out to irrigate, I heard something coming down the road boomety-boom, boomety-boom. That team come running by with the tubs flying up and hiting them on the rear end. I couldn't see them, but it sounded like a runaway up on the road.

Well, Todd was out in the corral milking his cows, and he seen his team go by with these tubs. They had probably run a mile and a half by then, and they was getting winded, so the tubs were going at a slower boompety-boom, boompety-boom. They kept on past where Pauline's sister and her husband, Joe, lived. Joe seen the team go by just trotting, because they had run about three miles by then. The old tubs was hitting the ground with a thud-thud-thud.

Todd got on his saddle horse to go after his team. He goes up to Joe and asks if he seen his team, and Joe said, "Yeah, they went over the hill." So Todd rides up the hill and meets his team, all lather and sweat, just jogging along and thinking they better come home. But the tubs was still going thump-thump, and that scared Todd's fresh saddle horse. He took off down the road with Todd a-pulling, but he couldn't hold him, so he run him clear home. After a while, the old team came into the yard, played out.

Todd could have got hurt, but he didn't, and we all laughed about it. He never said anything to me, but I heard through the grapevine that I got the blame for putting the tubs on that team.

My two big saddle horses, Red and Ribbon, were the first two horses I ever owned. They was probably eight or nine years old and had never been worked, so I started driving them around hitched to a wagon, and got them going, and Pauline's dad loaned me a team and another horse, so I put them old saddle horses in with the good team, and I could get by with them. I disced some ground, and harrowed some. A disc breaks up the ground after plowing and a harrow smooths it out and breaks up chunks of manure. It was kind of a wet April, and I had time to get their shoulders hardened up before we went to haying. And I broke them to work on buckrakes, and mowing machines, and what have you.

Then a guy lent me an old balky horse, called Gray, and said to use him if I could work with him, or he'd send him to a killer market. This horse had been beaten, and he was nervous. When balky horses are hooked up to something, they'll make big lunges and then fly back, but they won't pull anything. They'll crowd over against the next horse, and try to tangle him up, and they'll get rubbed into the lines. They'll do all sorts of things.

So, I hooked him up to the buggy with Bird, a well-broke buckskin mare that belonged to Pauline's dad. I'd get in the buggy and set there, and wouldn't speak to Gray or do anything—just set there. He'd stand there, scared and trembling, thinking I was going to whip him. After a little while, I'd unhook him and drive him off. I hooked him up like that for a day or two, and let him stand there, and he wouldn't move except for a big jump every once in a while. But, Bird wouldn't start on a jump.

Finally, he found out I wasn't going to whip him or scream at him, and he'd stand pretty good. After I done that for maybe two days, I hooked him up again and tapped old Bird so she'd start pulling the buggy. Gray would make a big lunge, but the buggy was going, and he'd get to trotting along following the old horse. I drove him around, and stopped him a time or two, and kept playing with him that away, and then started working him on a disc with four other horses. For a while, he'd bounce and hit the ground, but the other horses would keep coming, and I didn't fight him. Before the summer was over with, I was mowing with him, and working him on a buckrake with a horse on each side.

His owner was kind of a horse trader. He brought a fellow out one day when I was working Gray on the mowing machine. He said, "This horse used to balk, but Ray seems to get along with him." Of course, the horse was used to me by that time. Horses was cheap then, and the guy bought Gray for about $25, but the deal was that I could keep him 'til I got done haying.

When this guy took Gray home for some fall plowing, the horse balked, and reared up, and tore up the harness. His owner probably hit him with a whip, and that made the horse go into fits. The guy couldn't do nothing with him. Of course, a plow pulls harder, but if he had used the technique I did, I think he could have plowed with him. I had the patience to fool with him, and I didn't fight him. It's just one of those things. You get a horse figured out.

Horses are like people. What works on one won't work on another; some you can slap around and get their attention, and others you've got to use kindness to get them to work for you. Horses are smart. When you're breaking a horse to ride and to work, you've got to figure him out and keep ahead of him.

Pauline and I lived in a little bunkhouse with a cookstove, and a little cupboard, and a place for a bed, and that was about all. We packed in water from the outside. Our first child, Shirley, was born July 14. Pauline was laying down sick all day, but we thought we could put it off for the next day, so I could finish irrigating. Along about evening, we figured we'd better drive into town, and we wasn't there over about an hour 'til Shirley was born.

Pauline was in the hospital eleven days, and then we brought Shirley back to our little shack. They put her on canned milk, but she couldn't keep it down and was kind

Ray Holmes with Shirley, at Hublitz place.

of sickly, so old Doctor Dolan said she should have cow's milk. I never had no money to go out and buy a milk cow, but Pauline's dad lent us a two year old Hereford heifer that had calved late.

A cowboy's theory was that he wouldn't milk a cow: he didn't want milk on his boots. I guess I'm not the cowboy that most of them are, because I really don't mind to sit down and milk out a pail of milk. So I'd rope that heifer, and tie her to a fence, and milk out a little half-gallon bucket of milk morning and night, and that's the way Shirley grew up—on wild cow milk. We didn't have refrigeration, so Pauline would put the bucket of milk in cold water and set it in the window, and change the water two or three times a day. Pauline has always been a worker, and she canned up a lot of stuff that summer. We had big gardens and raised watermelons. We never had no money and never went anywhere. We just stayed home.

Nowadays, I don't have the feed to take care of milk cows, and I'm getting older and lazy: I hate to have to go get a cow. But we've usually had a cow around. I couldn't have a cow that would give a lot of milk, though, because I couldn't be there all the time to milk. And if you try to put a second calf on a cow, sometimes a cow doesn't take two calves very well. If you were gone, the second calf might not get to suck. In a dairy, you have a certain time to milk, night and morning, but my calves suck the cow, and I just milk when I get around to it.

We was there in that little bunkhouse until October, when we went down home, and I took a job on a ranch twenty miles out of Moorcroft. I was happy. It was cold, and I rode and fed cattle and never thought anything about it. The ranch belonged to Emma McKean, and she ran about 400 head of cows. It was a one-man operation, except for haying. In good winters, they didn't feed anything but cottonseed cake to those cows. They had feed bunks, like troughs, scattered up the river, and I'd go a-horseback calling the cows, and they'd be there about the time I'd come along. I'd feed so many cows at a bunk and keep on riding. I'd leave on the dot of 7:00, and it'd be 2:30 or 3:00 in the afternoon before I would come back and eat. So my whole day was caking cows, seeing that the water was open, and I had to wrangle about 100 head of replacement heifer calves first thing of a morning and feed them cake, too. Then, I had a hospital bunch of thinner cows right at the house—twenty-five or thirty head. It was a nice open winter with a lot of grass, and we never fed a spear of hay all winter.

It was a good job. We got $50 a month. It don't sound like much today, but we had a nice little warm house with one bedroom, a living room, a kitchen and a porch. It was furnished, and our utilities were paid, and we got milk and eggs from the ranch. We made butter from our share of the milk and sold some of that.

Emma McKean never had anybody to take care of the chickens before, so I took care of them, too. Even if you only keep a few chickens, you got to keep the chicken house clean with clean straw on the floor, and keep plenty of feed and water in front of the chickens. I used to water my chickens twice a day.

In winter, you got to keep the place warm so the hens don't freeze their combs and stop laying. I always took warm water out for them in the morning, and I've seen times when it'd be icy and froze up at noon, and I'd have to clean their pen out and give them some more warm water. It may sound funny for a cowboy, but there is nothing I like to do more of a morning after breakfast than take a little warm pail of water down and feed the chickens. Or some Saturday, when I wasn't busy, to clean the chicken house all out and put in fresh straw. The chickens will sing and fly, because they're really happy then. I always had the chickens a-laying!

In later years I got a neighbor who believes in keeping her chickens until they die of old age. Two and three year old hens do lay, but she has a lot of gold-brickers in the bunch that she feeds for nothing. Chickens was put on this earth for us people to eat, so you might as well eat them as let them die of old age.

Along in spring when it warmed up at the McKean ranch the bedbugs thawed out, and Shirley got bites all over her. We had to take all the canned goods out and go over to stay with Mrs. McKean for 24 hours while we fumigated. At that time, you put cyanide balls in every room, and closed up the windows, and went out and shut the doors. Afterward, you'd throw open the doors and let the fumes out.

We had a tractor to mow with, but the haying machinery was in bad shape. I had four boys—just kids—to work with, and it was hard work, because I had to take all the heavy end of it. I got disgusted trying to get the hay up with that kind of a deal. Pauline cooked the noon meal for all of us, and the kids would eat the other two meals with Mrs. McKean, but she wanted us to board the boys cheaper than what we could manage. We didn't have to leave, but we pulled out and come back to Sheridan with our few belongings piled in the back end of our '32 Chevy convertible coupe. That ranch is now under water by the Keyhole Dam.

We went to Teunis Clark's on Wolf Creek in August. Pauline went to cooking, and I worked in the hayfield driving a buckrake, putting up second-cutting hay. We fenced thirty-eight big hay corrals with posts and wire that fall, and it was a lot of work. I took care of the chickens, milked the cows, mowed some lawn, repaired fences, built corrals, stacked hay, and done a little of everything. When you come in late man on a job that way, you do a lot of the odd-and-end work.

I never rode there except for going up one time to the Freeze Out Cowcamp the first of September. A lot of men went up to gather cattle, and the first night there we got fourteen inches of snow. They'd already killed a beef and hung it in a tree, and the next morning we had steak off it for breakfast. They talk about aging beef, but it was good meat that next morning.

It snowed all day and night, and the next day we couldn't ride. Teunis got worried about how things were with the cattle down below, so I come off the mountain and come home. It was broken clouds in the mountain with fourteen inches of snow, but when I got out to the face of the mountain and looked off into the valley, it had rained down around Dayton, and I rode right out into bare ground and sunshine.

We left Clark's the first of December, because they thought Pauline's cooking was too expensive, and we stayed around Sheridan for a month, living in a tourist camp. Then, we went back down home because I couldn't find anything to do, and we was using up my money. We lived in my uncle Clyde's house until the third Christmas we were married. Then, about the first of March, Trusty Moore wanted me to go look after some Mexican steers at the D ranch. But the outfit sold in May, and they brought in their own men. That let me out, so I went to the LA ranch.

We were visiting over at Pauline's folks' place when we heard the flash on the radio about Pearl Harbor.

We couldn't believe it and thought maybe it was a prank. Then everybody got excited and set down by the radio, and it was real. We had been bombed, and we was into war.

In town next day, all you could hear about was the war and how quick the United States was going to whip the Japs. Some older guys had gone for a year's training, and they thought they was home free in a day or two, but they got their notices to stay in the service. Troops was on the move, and they speeded up the draft and took men off these ranches really fast. They pulled a troop train out of Sheridan full of enlisted men that went to the 115th Cavalry. Boys would get to drinking in town and go and sign up for the Army. There was a slug of ranch boys went right out on that first train.

At twenty-seven, I would have been eligible for the draft. I was 1A when I registered, but I was married, and we had Shirley, and they backed men like that up a little. Then, I was right up on the firing line to be drafted when they backed up the age limit. If I had been single, I would have been in the service, because they was taking them up to 30 years old, and I'd have wanted to go. But when you're married, you don't want to go off and leave your family. You could get deferred, too, if you was working on a ranch, but I never had to put in for any deferments.

So the way it ended up, I was in between the two wars—too young in World War I and too old in World War II.

CHAPTER NINE

SOME TALK ABOUT HERD MANAGEMENT

It takes a lot of time and work to keep a bunch of cattle well sorted. You should cull commercial heifers in the spring after you've wintered, before you put them with a breeding herd, and then again in the fall, because they'll change by fall. Then you should cull them once more when they calve. To do it right, you should keep working them clear on to where their calves are on the ground. You have to keep getting rid of the poorer ones. But that would all be quite a program, and you would have to spread it over a number of years.

To build up a good herd starting with heifer calves, you should really mother up every calf and look them over for conformation to see if that's the type of cattle you want. You would be working for a uniform bunch of cows—good, straight-bodied cows with good backs, long hips and loins and heads, and good legs under them. You would be shooting for cows more or less the same size. I would shoot for what I call middle-of-the-road cattle—not overly big cows, and not little cows, cows that would weigh in the neighborhood of 1,050 to 1,150 pounds when they're dry. A great big cow up to 1,300 or 1,400 pounds won't generally have as good a calf as a cow that's in the middle, and a dry cow that would only weigh 850 or 900 pounds when she's fat, is not big enough when you

Cattle on summer range.

go to sell her. Middle-of-the-road cattle are best.

You should start with the heifers. If you put the bulls in with them for about forty days, and then take them out, and then pregnancy test, you better just sell any heifer that's not with calf. Usually they are shy breeders, and they will be that way for life. You'd sell a few good animals maybe, but if you sold them all you would be keeping your herd clean. You'd keep better uniformity in your cows. But, it's all up to what an individual wants to do with his herd.

If a cow has balloon teats, meaning great big teats, her heifer calf shouldn't go on as a replacement animal, because that's hereditary. Her calf, when he's little, can't get the teat into his mouth. And they're hard to milk, You can milk them teats down, and the cow will raise a calf, but most times a cow with big teats don't give very much milk.

If a cow had a cancer eye, you shouldn't save a replacement heifer calf off her. A little growth starts in the eye from a small spot, and it keeps on getting worse until it finally eats through the eye and destroys it.

Nowadays, the vets can take an eye out, if it's just a little spot. But to me a one-eyed cow is kind of bad in a bunch. She's likely to be timid. She may go ahead and produce, but if you can catch it when it's just a little thing, and get a good price out of the cow and replace her, you are better off.

People have said I had a wonderful ability when it comes to remembering cattle. But, that's the way you got to know them cattle and how they are producing. Anybody could go out here and pick out a nice, uniform, saleable bunch of cows, but if you are aiming to improve your herd, you've got to know it's not always a pretty cow that's producing.

Sometimes a poor-looking cow will produce good calves. Of course, you do work on looks, but that's not all of it. It's the same way with bulls. You try to pick a bull that's got good conformation, but he may not breed the same way he looks. Maybe some other bull hasn't got the looks, but he's producing better calves.

Really, when you buy a bull, you should look at his mother to see if she's got big teats, or something else wrong. But, you generally can't do that. I mean, you buy a bunch of range bulls when they are two years old, and how in the hell are they going to go out there and find the mothers? They ain't going to take that much time.

But, that is something to study.

There are fences to look after, and a steady rider always fixes some fence, and looks for stray cows, and keeps the bulls scattered. And when you're riding, you're looking out for any cow that may be producing a bad calf. You remember from last year that she didn't do so good, and you can figure that cow out. That's the way I do it.

A lot of times a guy will be a good stockman and knows cattle, but not be really what you would call a cowboy. Maybe he can't do much with a horse, and is no rider, but he knows cattle and how to take care of them. He may not be much of a cowboy other than just to ride a gentle horse. He just kind of rides around. It's pretty glorious to see a man just riding along on a horse, which a lot of times is very easy work, but you got to be a-thinking about your job, too.

In a range operation, the old cows are usually shipped at about ten years old. After that, their teeth get poor, and it's harder for them to rustle. If you've got plenty of feed, you can take them out and feed them more through the winter until they are eleven, but the next year you are going to have a lot of cows to get rid of. Usually, they are marked with the last digit of the birth year, so you always know their age.

There are cows that will keep producing at twelve and thirteen years. I've even seen cows fourteen or fifteen years old that have a big, fat calf. On the other hand, I've seen thin, shelly, seven and eight year old cows that are at the end of the line. They break and their calves are poor.

So, you can't just go in and say well, I'll take out all the ten year olds. Some people have to do it thataway when they don't have anyone that knows cows. On the other hand, if you cut at about ten all the time, you are keeping the old cows out.

One thing about solid-colored cattle, without white bellies, is that they won't snow burn on the udder and teats. The teats on black cows are black, and on red cows reddish or tan-colored, so they don't burn. Herefords have pink skin on their undersides. The big cows with big bags really get it worse, because their teats are so close to the ground. Two year old heifers with small bags can snow burn some, but nothing like the older cows.

If cows are in a corral, or under a shed, they don't snow burn because there is not enough snow there to reflect that bright ray. In a country with timber and stuff, they don't burn as badly, because they can get around trees or something. The first day after the sun breaks, out after a big storm, is when they burn. It's just like your face when it's bright and you snow burn. It's worst with fresh snow after a big storm. After the first day some of the fire goes out of it.

A snow-burned cows' teats get big scabs on the ends. Sometimes you have to rope the cows so you can grease the teats and clean the scab off. When you take that scab off, the teats bleed and get sore and then scab back over. You may have to help the calves suck, because the cows kick the calves off. The only times they get to suck is when you tie the cows up so they can't kick. After the first time they usually get going all right.

I remember one day when it was snowing, but there was a kind of bright ray coming from the sun. I never saw anything like it. I burnt my face 'til I couldn't shave for a week or two. I had to rub cream on my face, and it was pretty near solid scab. It was kind of a violet ray hitting your face and it was just a-burning. That was a day the cows burned. A lot of people knew it would happen and put their cows in corrals, but they got burned anyway.

Purebred cattle are used to produce breeding bulls for commercial herds. If you buy the right bull, and he crosses well with the cows, and produces good calves, that's what puts you in the purebred business. Breeding is important with commercial cattle, too, but you don't keep track of them as much. In a commercial herd, if you have a lot of bulls out, some will breed good and some bad, but you don't know which bull is which. That's why they keep raising purebred cattle—trying to produce proven bulls. To keep building up your herd all the time, you want bulls that are better than your cows. With the right purebred bulls, you know you are putting good blood back into your commercial herd.

Generally bulls run 1,600 or 1,700 pounds. Sometimes a bull will breed bigger than he is, or he can breed smaller. That has to be tried. They pick these good-looking bulls as herd sires, but there's a lot of bulls that don't breed the way they look. The herd sire is the top breeding bull that you buy if you are raising purebred calves. He's got a good pedigree that carries down along the line of cattle. Maybe he is a grandson of a great breeding bull, and the auctioneers make it sound like you're buying the very own son of this great bull that may have been dead for years. It's just like horse pedigrees. They start with a good pedigreed horse, and then the sons and daughters come right on down. So people get excited that they're getting bloodlines right up close. You think you're buying a daughter or a son of this great sire, and he could be several generations back.

When you buy a bull, most generally the herd sire is there. At a big sale, they lead the main herd sire through if he's got a lot of calves in the sale. They'll show the herd sire to the public—lead him around the ring and show him off. So you pick out the bulls, and check the papers, and they'll show you which bull they're sired by. There's a lot of bulls bought on the strength of the herd sire. People will like a bull, and then, looking at the herd sire, they'll say, "Well, this bull resembles the old daddy."

Whenever you breed a Red Angus bull to a Hereford cow, you get a red brockle-face or a red baldy. A Black Angus and a Hereford produce a black baldy. Once in a while, you get one that looks like a Hereford, but the red strain is very strong. If you have a black bull that carries a red strain, and put it on a Hereford cow, you can still get some red calves. The red strain had to be strong because at one time, a hundred years ago, the black cattle was all red, and then they bred them to black. Now, some breeders have bred back to the reds again.

Angus bulls are naturally hornless. In a pasture, they will scuffle and fight. There may be several cows in heat, but the bulls will all be chasing one cow and fighting. Horned bulls don't do that so much. You'll see them bunch up a little, but pretty soon there is a big fight and then the bulls scatter. Where they do cross breeding, they'll run horned bulls in with Angus bulls, and that automatically makes the bulls scatter, because the Angus are afraid to bunch with horned bulls. I've seen Angus bulls walking through a bunch, and a big old horned bull will come along, and the Angus are scared of him. He will make a run at them, and he's just bellering, "Get the hell out of here!"

If you bring in a strange bull, and he has just one other bull to fight, maybe he could whip his way and be boss. But, if he is the only strange bull, the others will double-team on him and whip him out. If you drive bulls, you can soon figure out which bull's the big boss in the outfit. All he has to do is turn his head and another bull moves away from him. Some of the other bulls may fight among themselves, but the king pin don't have much trouble fighting.

When boss bulls get older—seven or eight, say—and they get whipped out, they go off and stay by themselves. That's about the end of them. When that happens, they are useless for breeding cows.

About twice in my lifetime, when I was young, my dad had bulls that wouldn't stay home, and he'd tie boards over their eyes to keep them with the cows. Maybe we'd bring one in to breed the milk cows, and it would be slow business for the bull around there, and he'd want to pull out, you know. With the board over his eyes for a couple of weeks, he would get located. It worked like blinders do.

What you do is this: you use a board better than a foot long and about a foot wide, so that it sticks out six inches or so on either side of the bull's head; you bore two holes in it, about the width of his head, and put a rope through the holes and take it around his horns. That way, it drops down over his eyes. The bull can see to get around, because when he looks straight down, he can see the ground. But, when he walks up to a fence sideways and turns to jump straight over, it looks dark because of the board. And cattle are afraid to jump into anything they can't see. I have used this board trick on Mexican steers, and it worked. They never got away from me.

Mexican steers like to hunt up cows. They have that "bulling instinct," and that's why they're called "bulling steers." Some of them are probably castrated late, when they're too old. Anyway, they'll jump fences. They can just walk up to a four-wire fence and jump it. You can't hardly fence for them. So, if they ever locate with a bunch of cows, you have to drive them out, and if you don't put them somewhere they can't jump out of, they'll just go back. They can even breed a cow sometimes, and she will have a Mexican calf.

They'll even jump on another steer and start riding him, and the steer gets to running, and they keep jumping on him, and sometimes they can kill one that way—just play him out. A lot of little outfits run heifers and steers together, and a bulling steer will ride a heifer, too. If they're all used to running together they don't cause much trouble, but sometimes a strange steer will get in. And if one heifer would get in with, say, a hundred steers or so, they would probably ride her to death. I saw a registered cow one time that got in with about 500 Mexican steers, and they rode her and killed her. We found her dead—they just kept after her. It was exhaustion, that's what it was. With so many steers chasing her, she got too hot, and played out, and she died.

You run a bull for two years, and if he don't turn out to be a good bull, you send him to market and take a baloney price for him. You could run a steer up till he's two years old for about half what you could run a two year old bull, because you can kick steers out in the pastures, while bulls has got to be fed more. They've got to be kept around, and somebody has to watch over them and the fences and stuff.

Older bulls don't cover the country like younger bulls. They tend to lay around the water hole and wait for the cows to come in. If you watch, you can usually tell the old bulls and pick them out yourself. If you was riding all the time, and saw an old bull staying off by himself, why you'd figure he wasn't a breeding bull, so you'd probably think about getting rid of him. The old bulls go for baloney. The buyers like the older bulls that are kind of thin in the fall. They pay a good price per pound for them—more money than for a fat, two year old bull. I don't know why; I think the meat is probably more tasty.

The value of crossbreeding has to do with hybrid vigor. The first cross of two breeds like Hereford and Angus—or any two breeds—is bigger and better than the parents. Then, if that animal is crossed back either way to Hereford or Angus, you are going back to the same breed. If you take an Angus-Hereford cross and breed back to an Angus bull, you are going back to the Angus side, so you will not have as good a gaining animal as you have in the first cross. Then, you can throw in a third breed such as Shorthorn or Charolais.

The exotic breeds haven't been used for too many years. Charolais are big, white cattle. If you breed them to an Angus cow, you have to pull about all the calves. Mexicans are kind of slim, lanky cattle, and I guess their heads must not be so big. With the Mexican bulls that they bring in now, they claim that heifers calve real easy. Simenthal cattle have white on them. They look like exotic cattle, but they are not as enormous as some. I don't know why people started wanting bigger cattle. I guess they thought they would get cattle with more meat on them. This new generation wants to experiment to get bigger cattle, but when they are enormous like that, it takes more feed to get them finished out. At least, that's my idea of it.

There is a lot of Longhorn cattle around, and people rent the bulls out. They even bring them in here from

Oregon. You just rent them for the summer. After they get older, they get pretty big, but their calves are small and long-legged. They use a lot of them for roping calves.

Right now the major breeds are Hereford and Angus. I don't know of any big herds of exotic cattle, though there are a lot of crosses. I really think the best cross is Hereford and Angus. It seems to take something from both sides, and give them the hybrid vigor to where they are good gaining cattle, that finish out just about right from 1,200 to 1,250 pounds with good red meat on them.

Somewhere along the line, they introduced "polled" Herefords. I don't know how it started. A polled Hereford is the same as another Hereford, but without horns. They call them muleys and they are round-headed when they're born. They never do grow horns. There must have been a freak that somebody picked up, because you breed a polled bull to a horned cow, and they will have a lot of muley calves, although some of them throw back and have horns. Sometimes, they would have scurs—little loose, curled horns. The Polled Association was very strict about scurs on cattle. If you was showing a bull, and he had scurs, you was supposed to leave them on. But, some guys would cut them off so no one would know.

When you put an Angus bull on a Hereford cow, you get mostly polled (or muley) calves. I would say there might be less than a third with horns from an Angus bull. But, polled cattle have never been as popular in this country as horned cattle. Both horned and muley cows have advantages. When you feed protein blocks, you're better off with muley cattle. Muleys run by themselves do better without the horned cows. Horned cattle can't be fed as many in a bunch. Whenever you've got one or two horned cows in a bunch of muleys, you know where the boss cows is. If there's any feed around, the horned cows are eating and the muley cows are standing back.

Horned bulls have some advantages, also. Polled bulls have a tendency to get together in the pasture. They scuffle and fight, but they don't hurt each other, so they won't get out and scatter. Horned bulls fight, and the younger bulls are scared of the old ones, and they are a lot better breeding bulls than polled bulls, because they scatter out in the hills, and get over the country. There is bulls here and there, each with a little bunch of cows, scattered around. If they stay along the creeks and fight, and the cows is out grazing, there is no bull with them. That's the big problem with Angus—getting them to scatter. Say you have 400 head of cattle in a pasture, and six bulls to a hundred—If they're Angus, you've got to have somebody riding and scattering them, because they will bunch up. I've never been around that many polled Herefords, but I've been told they are the same as Angus when it comes to bunching up, because they don't have horns, either.

When you sell your calves, they usually weigh around 350 to 400 pounds. Of course, the buyers will take lighter calves, especially if they've got good wheat crops in Kansas to graze on them on. One thing that makes a lot of difference in the price is how much feed is available. For a few years, when buyers had lots of feed, they wanted lighter calves, and there was a five cent spread between the little calves and the big ones. If you was offered forty cents a pound for your bigger calves, the lighter calves—300 to 350 pounds—would be about forty-five cents.

I think the day of light cattle going into the feed lot and right up on grain is over with. Some people use silage, but the fellow that buys my calves takes them down in the fall of the year and runs them through the winter on some corn stalks and hay—about the way we do. Then, he lets them go onto good pasture for a while before putting them in the feed lot, somewhere around the first of August. I had two or three light calves last fall, and I never sold them, because calves was going through the sale ring real cheap. Nobody wanted to put all that feed in them.

Buyers will contract a price on calves in June or so, and they'll agree to a delivery date between the 15th of October and the 1st of November, and you're supposed to deliver them on that date. There's another way to go, though, and that's to hold your calves without a contract and sell them for whatever they are worth the day you deliver them. Some years, you would do better to hold your calves because the price in the fall turns out better than the price in June. But by contracting in June, you get what you contracted for even if prices drop by fall.

There is such a thing as buyers contracting a lot of cattle and going broke. They contracted a lot of cattle, and the prices went down so much they couldn't get their money back. I've seen cattle high the first of September, and by November the price had slipped a nickel, or a dime, or maybe even more than that. So, it's all a gamble when you sell.

CHAPTER TEN

THE FORTIES

The D Ranch sets on Prairie Creek in pretty much open country with no trees around. In my time, there was a long old log house with two bedrooms, a kitchen, a living room and dining room. The place was kept up, but it was all log buildings and nothing fancy. Trusty Moore managed the estate. There was 600 head of Mexican steers and two guys working there that couldn't get the feed out to them. Trusty Moore told me and another guy that he'd take us on, and when we put out all the hay them steers could eat, we could sit in the house the rest of the day. So, we would feed and be done by two o'clock. That's what we did from the first of January up into March, and there wasn't much snow, so we didn't have to put out too much hay.

The ranch was up for sale when I got there, but Trusty didn't think it would sell because land wasn't moving. But, then land started to move and the place was sold, and so I was only there for three months. The new owner brought his own hands.

The LA Ranch was right next door to the D Ranch, and it turned out they needed a married man that would stay around. Pauline and I didn't have much stuff to move at that time. Shirley was about three, and we just about made the move in our little car.

They didn't have electricity at the LA then, and we did the washing there on a washboard. But then Pauline

Ray and Pauline Holmes, 1941.

and her dad went to Sheridan and come back with our first washing machine—a Maytag with a gas motor.

The LA was owned and run by Buster and Patsy Brown, who were brother and sister, and their mother. The place was between 15,000 and 20,000 acres. I rode some colts and built a lot of fence. The Browns only ran about 250 head of cattle, and they contracted out the hay, but one of my jobs was to rake it with a team and sulky rake.

Patsy had registered Morgans and some grade horses as well. Her father, L.A. Brown, had come to Spearfish, South Dakota with a trail herd from Texas. L.A. Brown's wife came from Mississippi, and when they moved here she thought she was getting a new house, but it was only a log cabin about twelve by fourteen feet, thrown together during the winter by some cowhands with saws and hammers. It had a dirt floor and dirt roof with cactus growing on it. And the windows was all crooked. I remember Mrs. Brown saying she sure was disappointed.

L.A. Brown died when I was small. He must have been a lot older than Mrs. Brown, and maybe that's why she always called him "Mr. Brown." Their old original cabin is restored now and on display over at the Carter Coal Company in Gillette. I guess Patsy donated it to them.

Buster Brown was a very fine fellow, but he had epileptic spells. He'd go along a week or two just fine, and then get a spell. He'd kind of sink away, and moan, and fall on the ground. Mrs. Brown and Patsy told me not to let him drive the binder, because they was afraid he would get hurt. Well, one day we was working together, and Buster was supposed to do the shocking, but he wanted to run the binder, so I let him.

Pretty soon I saw he'd throwed the binder out of gear and was setting up on the front of it hollering at the horses. They was out of control, mashing down grain as they went. I got in front of him and stopped him, talking to him and talking to the horses, got ahold of the lines, dropped the tugs, and got Buster laying down in the shade. He'd had a spell, and he laid there, kind of sleeping, 'til noon. There's a lot of gears in a binder, and if he had fallen, it would have wrapped him up in there and cut his legs off. The team would have got scared to death with him screaming and probably killed him.

Patsy and I rode through that mashed down grain later on, and she was wondering why it was all down. I told her I'd got the binder out of gear, and that the team got to going with me, and I was the one who mashed it down. I had to lie about that, because I shouldn't have let Buster get on the binder at all.

That summer we had a grass fire right there on the LA. It was nighttime, and I was turning the cream separator, and, WHAM! lightning hit, and I seen the fire start. It headed right for the LA buildings, rolling along with the wind. Mrs. Brown got on the telephone and called for help, and, of course, the neighbors come, but they couldn't get there right away with a fire engine. So we got out there with wet sacks, and the wind whipped around to a different direction, so we was able to save the buildings.

But the fire took on down into a meadow, and when the grass is dry, a grass fire can travel faster than a horse can run. It burned up about 50 tons of hay and one haystack that we had just finished that day. It burned to Prairie Creek, and jumped the creek, and started up the hill to the horse pasture. No one could get to the lead of the fire, so they told me to go open the horse pasture fence on the other side, and let out the horses in there. By the time I got there in the dark, there was no sign of the fire, and my first thought was that the fire had beaten me to it and gone on. But I got off my horse and felt the ground, and grass was still there. We were lucky—the fire burned out when it got into thin grass on top of the hill.

We stayed at the LA for about a year, living in that little log house that's now over at the coal company in Gillette. It was five miles to get the mail, and I sometimes went for it in a buggy. That log house was so little all it took was the cookstove to keep it warm, although there were times in the winter when it would get real cold at night. At Christmas, we had a little Christmas tree, and we got Shirley a tricycle. She was three years old. She woke up about four o'clock Christmas morning and there's that tricycle, so she jumps right on, and I can see her yet jumping right back off! She never thought how cold that metal seat would be.

Our kids had big times at Christmas, but didn't get very much stuff. Nowadays, kids get so much they just keep opening packages and piling up paper, and by the time the day is over, they're going around looking for something old to play with.

By 1943, my dad wanted me to come and be close to him, because my brother was in the service, and my folks didn't drive a car. So in April, I went to work at the Ike Ranch which was nearby. The Ike Ranch was a good place, and a real pretty one, along the Belle Fourche River. Earl Ike had made money in the plumbing business in California, and he bought three ranches and put them together into about 12,000 acres, so even then it wasn't very big. But, he fixed the place all up and put up some new buildings, and insulated the old house and made it all modern. He ran Herefords, a cow and calf operation, and kept the calves until they was yearlings.

When we moved, I gave some neighbors ten bucks to haul our stuff over in a truck, and the truck wasn't near full because we didn't have much. We'd been living in a one-room house, and we had our clothes and our washing machine, but there were no stoves to move or anything like that.

My job was pretty much straight riding. One of the things I did was help trail about 300 head of cattle to Moorcroft, which should have been a four-day drive, but a cattle buyer had offered Ike an extra two cents per pound if we could deliver the cattle in three. There was me; Pete Jensen from the Devils Tower Hereford Ranch next door, with some of their cattle; Bob Scannadore, who was boss of the Ike Ranch; and a half-breed Indian named John Claymore.

Well, we got down by Moorcroft and put the cattle in on the river, so they'd get water, and Scannadore says, "Nothing to do now but lay and rest," so he unsaddled his horse. He was already figuring up the extra two cents a pound. But Claymore and I knew that when the first freight train come through, things would pick up, so we kept our horses saddled and rode up to the top of a knoll, where we could see it a-coming.

When cattle hear a train coming, they get curious and walk toward it, but when it whistles at a crossing, they will bust right out back the other way. That's just what happened. The train came along, and the cattle walked toward it, kind of curious with their heads in the air—and then the guy jerked that whistle and the cows came back at a run.

Scannadore wasn't saddled up, and I believe Jensen had gone uptown, so there was just the two of us. My horse wasn't fast enough to outrun the lead steer, and that's what you've got to do, but Claymore's horse was faster, and he caught the lead just before they hit a three-wire fence, and he got them all to milling around, and we was able to wrap them up. That was about as near as I ever came to getting into a stampede. In the old days, they'd shoot the lead steer if they couldn't outrun him.

So anyway, we weighed the cattle and sold them to the buyer. We had trailed them so far and so fast that we knocked enough weight off them so that buyer could afford the extra two cents! Of course, he knew that was the way it would work out. A lot of times a buyer will jump the price a cent or so a pound, if he knows you wool your cattle a lot, which means to handle or move them around, and get a lot of shrink. You may think you are making money, but the buyer knows better.

Scannadore had worked with Ike as a plumber in California, and we got along fine, even though he didn't know too much. But older hands are always thinking up pranks for someone who's green. One day, we was de-horning cattle and Scannadore had throwed his new chaps over the fence—one leg on each side. They was rough-side-out chaps, kind of white colored, and we was cutting off horns and letting the blood just paint one leg red. When Scannadore went to get them, God was he mad! He had one leg nice and white, and the other blood red, and he never did get the blood off those chaps.

It don't matter how well you are liked when you're a green hand. The older guys are going to have some fun with you, and you have to learn some things the hard way. When a new hand comes to a ranch, there will be leftover horses that nobody else wants to ride, and when he goes out to ride one, everyone is going to be watching him, waiting for him to make a mistake.

My theory was not to seem to know too much—just to do the best you could until you got to be in with the older bunch. When a guy starts telling about all the horses he has rode, and what he can do, he soon gets his air tested. Even if you're a pretty good hand, the others will come up with something to test you. They'll put you on a bad horse, or send you out on a hard roping job, or set you after a cow that's tough to get, and then when you don't make it, they'll razz you for saying what you could do.

If you never say you can do anything, they haven't got no comeback.

If four or five men are against you, they'll run you out. You might as well pack your bag, because they'll make everything so disagreeable you'll wish to Christ you had left. A crew of men is like a bunch of horses. They can turn on a strange one who isn't acclimated. They are all good guys, and they'd do anything for you most of the time, but you've got to prove yourself.

Rationing was on then, and lots of people laid in big supplies of sugar and coffee before it happened. The government sent out questionnaires, and you was supposed to say what supplies you had and turn them in, but if you didn't, you could turn around and sell them for a good price on the black market. People knew it was black market, but if they needed coffee or sugar, they would buy it even at double the price. I don't suppose coffee was over fifty cents a pound if it was that, so if you paid a dollar a pound for it, it would still have been cheap compared to today.

Gasoline was rationed on ranches, and a guy like me with a car was only allowed ten gallons a month without ration stamps. We had a gas washer, and it seems to me we got about five gallons of gas for that. You had to have your tires checked and the numbers on them taken down, so that if you bought a new tire, a tire dealer had to see if you really needed a new one. Then, he'd write down the number of the tire you were turning in.

We didn't have to bother with meat stamps. On an outfit with men working, every man was allowed some sugar for canning. Goldie Hardy was ranch cook on the Ike Ranch, and she'd put all the men's sugar allowances in a big jar, and you could dip into it for cereal or whatever. What was left over in a month, she would use to make pie or cake for the men.

Goldie raised chickens. Of course, they was Ike's chickens, but she looked after them like they was her own. Well, one day Pauline and I was up visiting my folks, and along comes Ike with a jug, and we all got to drinking. He told us to come down to his place and we'd have a chicken fry. Goldie had gone to town, and when we gets down to Ike's place, he goes for the .22 and starts shooting. He was drunk, but he hit the chickens clean through the head and stacked them up. I'd hate to have him shoot at me that way!

So Pauline cleaned the chickens, and we were in the middle of a big chicken fry when Goldie comes home from town. She had worked hard raising those chickens, and things hit the fan. She might just have worked there, but she sure told Ike where to set his empties!

Ike could be good to work for, but when he'd start sobering up after a drunk, he had a real mean streak. He'd be drunk for a day or two, and then come back and everything was wrong. He'd chew everybody out and get real tough. One morning, I was fifteen minutes late coming for the fencing crew after a three-mile ride to get there. We'd had a set-to before that, and I'd already told him he'd better quit jumping onto me when he was drunk, but he did it again that morning. So I quit right there. It was the middle of September in 1944—about two weeks after our son, Charles, was born.

Charles was delivered by Dr. Clarenbaugh in Sundance, Wyoming, in an old house they called a nursing home. It was September 3rd, 1944, and I was out forty miles from Sundance. I don't know how I got the word, because we didn't have a telephone out in that country, but I went along to see him in the evening. My mother went with me that first time I saw Charlie Boy. He was named Charles Eugene, after me and my brother both. The names Charles was handed down from my grandad, Charles Holmes, and I was named after him.

So we brought Charles home to the Ike Ranch for approximately two weeks when I quit, and we had to load him up, a tiny baby, and move on. He was a good baby, and his little sister, Shirley, was proud of him.

From the Ike Ranch, we went up to my folks' place to see if I could put together a deal to get my own place going. I would have liked to lease my folks' place in my own name, because that would have given me a chance to get some FHA money and a few cows. But, my dad had some of the place leased out on shares. He didn't understand that if I got the lease, he could still run some cattle, and I could have run some, built up from there. On my own, I couldn't get enough cattle with the credit I had. I would still have had to hire out some of the time, and that's no good when you're trying to run your own place.

So, there wasn't much future there for me. After six or eight weeks, I heard they wanted someone over at the Devils Tower Hereford Ranch. John Claymore had quit, and Pete Jensen asked me to work for him. There was only a one-room house to live in, but it was a fairly good-sized room, and I decided to go. The ranch was owned by Carl Steiger. He'd made his money with Deltox Rugs in Oshkosh. I think I got paid $125 a month. Pete would slip me some meat from the ranch, and he gave me a cow, so we had plenty of milk.

Charles got the croup so bad there, and it was fifty miles to Belle Fourche, or forty to Sundance. We were worried about him and didn't know what to do, but Pete Jensen had a boy that had had the croup, and Pete came over one night with a steamer. He fixed a tent over Charles, and put this steamer in there with camphorated oil, and in a little bit, the croup loosened up, and Charles was able to go ahead and breathe. So then we bought a steamer, and for the first two winters we had Charles, he would wake up every once in a while and give that awful cough, and get tightened up, and we'd have to steam him.

At the Devils Tower Hereford Ranch, I come up against the first cow I couldn't drive. One warm afternoon, Pete Jensen sent me to get a big old cow that wasn't bringing any calves. I went up to her and worked and worked, but couldn't drive her off the feed ground. I even roped her and tried to drive her ahead of me, but she wouldn't go, so I gave up and came back down to the ranch.

I knew Pete thought I had done something wrong. Next morning, the two of us went after her. We both worked and worked with this cow, but we couldn't get her away from there. Finally, we went and got a tractor and what they call a stone boat—a rig you can skid across the ground. We roped the cow, got her down, tied her legs together, and rolled her onto the stone boat. We drug her into the corral with the tractor and then hauled her into the sale ring.

Another time, we had a bull on the end of a rope and we had to get him through a gate. Well, he was too big to pull with a horse, so I goes up behind him and beats him and twists his tail, and through the gate he goes. But he's riled up, and I had to get my rope and hondue loose. A hondue or honda has a metal loop for the rope to slide through. I figured that when I jerked the rope off he'd walk away, but he snorted and took after me. I run down the draw with him right behind, and there's a log lying across the draw high enough so that bull could go under it. I was young and active, so I reached up and grabbed onto that log and swung up, and the bull went right under me. It took us a while to get him steered around and headed back into the pasture.

My teeth started getting bad before I was thirty. They was kind of chalky and wouldn't hold a filling. They didn't ache steady, but they'd kind of grind and irritate me all the time. So, while I was at the Devils Tower Hereford Ranch, I went to see Dr. Kane in Sheridan, and he said they all had to come out. So the first time, he pulled all my back teeth and left fifteen in front. Later, he took them out, too. I just sat in the chair, and he deadened the gums, pulled them all out, shoved a mess of new ones into my mouth, and told me not to take them out.

My mouth never swelled, or got sore, or anything. I was staying with a cousin of mine, and I goes back up town and had a couple of drinks of whiskey. Well, that knocked me right off the Christmas tree, and I slept all night. I didn't know you wasn't supposed to drink liquor when you've had drugs.

I never take them false teeth out, unless I have a sore or something, but once in a while I pull them out in my sleep. Pauline woke up one morning wondering what she was lying on, and there are my teeth, down by her butt. A neighbor of ours gets a kick out of the idea that my teeth were biting Pauline in the butt. Anyway, these have been better teeth to me than my old ones.

In March of '46, Pete Jensen became manager at a ranch down in Hartsel, Colorado. He wanted me to come along with him as cow foreman, so we all went. The ranch was owned by Cap McDaniel, an oil man from Texas. It was a big outfit with 5,000 sheep and a couple of thousand head of cattle. It was swampy land, and they did about everything with horses. They must have had 150 horses there, including the work horses, and I rode most of the time.

Shirley was six by then, and she'd already started at the Meade Creek School near Sheridan, so we wondered how we'd work it out at the ranch. They offered to rent a house for Pauline and the kids in Hartsel, a little old town with just a few buildings and a school, but that would have meant I'd have been twenty miles way off down country at the ranch most of the time. As it turned out, Pete Jensen left in June, and since the altitude at the ranch was bad for Charles' croup, we left the first of September and headed back for Sheridan.

Pete Jensen had got the job of County Agent there, and he put in a good word for me with Allen Fordyce, who owned the Bar 13 near Sheridan, and needed a man to feed registered bulls. So that's where we went next, and Shirley went back to the Meade Creek School, just as though she'd been away on a summer visit. I was always lucky some way or other.

We started at the Bar 13 in the fall of 1946, and I fed the bulls that winter. In the spring, I went to calving cows and hand-breeding them—riding after them night and

Ray on Easter Egg at the Bar 13 in 1948.

morning, and bringing them in to the bulls. I had to keep the bulls in and see that the fences wasn't torn down. The breeding program started about April and didn't finish until September.

The Bar 13 had a string of show cattle, and it was a lot of work to look after them. They'd be fed and grained in stalls in the daytime and turned out at night. The stalls all had to be cleaned up every night and new straw put in, and then next morning we cleaned the barn out with a wagon and team. When the string was getting ready for a show, the cattle had to be brushed every day, and trimmed up some, and washed, and their feet trimmed, and they had to be trained to stand and show.

That show string travelled all over the place, even to California. I never went as far as California, but we'd go by freight train to Denver, Great Falls, Billings, Casper, Douglas and Cheyenne. I put in thirty-five days one summer out with the show string, helping the main herder. We usually had a forty-foot stock car, and we'd build a deck above the cattle about half the length of the car. That's where you'd put your gear and that's where you'd sleep. By the time you got the decking up, there wouldn't be more than a foot and a half between the deck and the roof of the car, and man, that old tar on the roofs could get really hot! Sometime, you'd just have to get out. And when it rained, the rain came blowing in through the cracks and you'd get soaked.

It was a hobo life. You'd take your bedding, and feed, and a barrel of water, and some groceries, too, because the freight trains wouldn't always stop where you could get a meal. We'd generally get to a place three days before show day. We'd sleep in the barns, and that didn't bother me. After the first night or two, you'd get used to all the noise—even the fireworks they'd set off after the rodeo was over. One night in Billings, I was sleeping behind a yearling heifer that was in heat, and some way or other a bull got loose and slipped in and bred that heifer, and I never knew it 'til after it was over with. I woke just in time to see the bull getting off.

One time in Denver we stayed in a cheap hotel. It was a rough place where you wouldn't have wanted to stay unless you was with a bunch of stockmen. It was so shabby you could jerk the doors and the locks would fall off. I shared a room with the old Scotch herdsman, and when we went to bed, we put a chair up against the door. Well, we heard a hell of a screaming and commotion in the hallway, so the herdsman reaches up, pulls the chair away, snaps the lock, and sticks his head out to see what's going on. And here comes this naked woman down the stairs. She had been with some guy and her husband come into the hotel, kicked in the door, and throwed a gun on both of them. She just screamed and came right out from under her boyfriend, and there she was, out in the hallway without any clothes on. Somebody finally throwed her a coat, but that damned fool herdsman was lucky he didn't get his head blown off sticking it out like that to watch a naked woman!

In the mornings, we'd take a little sprayer and spray the cattle and brush their hair and curl it up. Then, we'd get them laying down in the deep straw, all graded from the biggest ones down to the littlest ones, and it looked really nice with the straw patted in square behind them. If it was real hot, we'd put an electric fan so that it would blow down over the cattle.

The show string business has changed a lot today. Everything moves by truck, not railroad, and the younger generation has took over 'til I don't know the fellows on the road nowadays. Most of the outfits that was in the registered cattle business are gone. Even the Bar 13 don't show anymore.

There's always characters on a ranch. On the Bar 13, there was Tubby Badgett and Swede Teague.

Tubby came to work when he was a green kid about sixteen. One time, we were treating a yearling heifer on the ground for an abscess, and Tubby comes walking up to watch. He walked right up into the heifer's hind feet, and she kicked him in the shins and knocked his feet from under him. "Jesus Christ," said Tubby, "I didn't know they could kick laying down!" He was as green as if he came out of Washington, D.C.

The older men had a lot of fun teasing Tubby. There was Jess Grant in the bunk house, a big, husky man who was deaf and dumb. He and Tubby had beds next to each other. One Sunday afternoon, Tubby was asleep with his feet over on Jess's bed. Well, Jess goes to lay down, and puts Tubby's feet off, and Tubby puts them right back on again. So, old Jess raised up, grabbed Tubby, reached into a pocket and pulled out a knife. Tubby thought he was really going to cut his throat.

That's when I walked in, and there was Tubby standing in the corner, as wild-eyed as a steer that's had the hell run out of him. Jess just sat there grinning, but Tubby always believed Jess had been serious, and he was mad at the rest of us because nobody helped him.

Tubby always called me "Old Holmely." For a time, he thought I was the meanest man in the world. The first time he saw me, I come riding in wearing a slicker and chaps, and my whiskers was long. "Who's that?" Tubby asks, and someone, probably Swede Teague, says, "Don't even speak to that feller, because he will cuss you out. He's an ornery son-of-a-gun. They keep him by himself because he can't get along with nobody." Well, of course, I wasn't living in the bunkhouse because I was living with Pauline and the kids, but for a while I played along and acted mean around Tubby.

Some of the boys told him that one day they was going to snap a rubber band on him the way you do to castrate a calf. "I'd just tear it off," Tubby said, but they told him it would be over too quick. All it had to do was snap down and that was it—you was castrated. "I'd shoot you bastards," Tubby told them, and he half believed they would do it.

So, one day I had the rubber band machine in my hip pocket, and I walk into the bunkhouse, and there is Tubby sound asleep across his bed with his legs spread out. I took out the machine and then reached down and grabbed him. He jumped up fighting and striking. "I'm going to kill you, Holmely!" he hollered. But Swede said, "It's too late. You already got a rubber band on." And Tubby stops and grabs hold of himself to look, and we all busted up laughing.

That's the way Swede Teague was. Around a bunch of men, he could always get something funny going. He was missing a finger, and he said a chicken et it. What happened was it got caught in a rope and snapped off, but he swore a chicken picked it up and et it. Swede was a good hand, but he liked whiskey, and he was always getting fired. Often, he would get hired back on.

I had to get him up in the middle of the night once to help move some cattle, and he was all drunked up and I couldn't find his gear. So, I put another feller's clothes on him, and someone else's chaps, and a big cap, and I poured some coffee into him and got him up on a saddle, and we set off about daylight. He didn't know what the hell he was doing. About noon, he lifts this big cap up over his eyes and says, "God! It's daylight out!"

Swede didn't care if he got fired. He'd go off and drink a little whiskey and then get another job. In the late 50s, he was at a ranch near Dayton. He and his boss, Bob

Barker, were leading their horses through one of those big culverts under the highway. Bob Barker's horse slipped and fell in the middle of that culvert, and they couldn't pull him out with the other horse. There was only a foot of water in there, but it doesn't take much to drown a horse. When they're down like that, they will go to banging their heads and snuff in enough water to drown. So, Barker sends Swede back to the ranch to get the jeep, while he sits there in the culvert holding the horse's head out of the water.

Well, Swede has to go through Dayton to get to the ranch. On his way back with the jeep, he stops for a beer. He's sitting at the bar, laughing, and McManus, who runs the place, says, "What's so funny?" And Swede tells him, "The boss is up there in the culvert, sitting in the water, holding this horse's head—and I'm drinking beer!" McManus thinks that's the best he ever heard, so he offers Swede another beer on the house. So, Swede has two before he goes on and he and Barker get the horse out.

About two months later, Swede was laying on his bed when Barker comes in and says, "Get your stuff together. I'm taking you to town." Swede knew Barker had probably stopped in the bar, and everyone had laughed about the time he'd been holding the horse's head up while Swede was in town drinking.

Swede was the one that said, "Never holler Whoa! in a tight place." It meant that when you're pulling with a team in a bad place, where you could get stuck, you'd better keep the load moving. But, Swede said it to me when he was pouring me a big shot of whiskey and I hollered, "Whoa!"

Swede worked here and there over the years, but when he got to the Bar 13, he stayed there until he died. He got cancer of the throat, and he's buried at Custer

Battlefield. They always said whiskey would get him, but his friend, Jack Reisch, said, "It just goes to show that whiskey won't kill you, but cancer will!"

When I started at the Bar 13, the old timers tried to get me just like everyone else. There was a mare in the corral they called Goldie, and she'd gotten big and fat, and she'd bucked off some of them farmer boys. So, one day they told me to take Goldie and trail some horses over to Dutch Creek.

Well, we wasn't to go for a couple of days, so I took Goldie down to my place, and put her in a muddy corral, and started working with her. I tied up one of her hind feet, and wooled her around, and turned her loose in there and rode her in the mud. The day before we went to Dutch Creek, I took her outside and galloped the hell out of her, and the next morning I rode her some more. Three of the ranch hands come down to see me bucked off. I drug Goldie out of the barn, with that old dry sweat on her, and they said, "Christ! You already rode her!" They probably *would* have seen me bucked me off if I'd got on her big and fresh, but by the time we started out for Dutch Creek, I had her under control enough to trail horses. I rode her a lot after that, and she never worried me. Oh, she could get a little humpy, but I could keep her straight.

The winter of '48 and '49 was thick with magpies. Magpies are a cannibal bird, black and white, with long tail feathers and long beaks. They will pick on cattle, and if they get blood coming, they will keep at it and wear an animal out. They'll eat on brands, too. If an old horse gets down, they'll start picking on his eyes and they'll eat him alive.

Poison will work on magpies, because they've got a stomach—not like a chicken that's only got a craw. You can't poison a chicken. One way is to bore a big hole down into a two by four, and fill it with poison tallow, and put it up on a barn somewhere, and you'll kill magpies. That winter, I found a dead calf, so I cut off a hindquarter, poked some holes in that fresh meat with a stick, and poured in some strychnine. I put the hindquarter in the cellar overnight to let the strychnine work through, and then I wired it on the barn. The magpies came sailing in, and we must have killed hundreds.

Nowadays, magpies are protected by environmentalists, but they really raise Cain with livestock in the winter. It's like coyotes. If man hadn't killed off the prairie dog and other animals they feed on, coyotes wouldn't bother livestock. Man has made a lot of the problems himself, but you've got to go along with the prairie-dog control program, or they eat up so much grass they'll take over your whole place. Man has to figure out some way to live, too. You have to make a choice, whether you're going to feed all these animals or feed people, so I don't know what the answer is.

We had another fire in the summer of '49. The fire got going, and then the wind started, and it burnt for several days. I stayed up one night to keep a lookout. It's a wonder the whole outfit didn't burn up, because the buildings were set close together, and if one had gone up, the rest would have gone, too.

The fire burned itself out, but the wind kept blowing. We was taking cattle over to Meade Creek, and when we got on top of the divide, and went to open a gate, the wind was blowing so hard it blew the bridle reins right out into the air. You couldn't hardly stand up in that wind. You could throw yourself into it and not fall over. It would just hold you.

When we came home that evening, Pauline had taken the children and gone. I was glad, because with trees blowed down, and with the threat of fire and that wind, you couldn't have saved anything if the house caught afire. The wind had blowed the chickens into kind of a porch, and they was setting there. And there was a shed set up on blocks that the wind blew all to pieces. It blew some roofs off the fairground grandstands and raised Cain at the airport. Lloyd Brown was setting in his house over on Meade Creek, reading, when a great big cottonwood crashed down and took the porch right off the house. A little further, and it would have taken him, too.

Talking about Lloyd Brown reminds me of a time he and I came by his place trailing cattle in cold weather. He had a fifty-gallon barrel of home-made wine, and he'd throwed in plums, and chokecherries, and blueberries, and I don't know what all. It was sour wine like they drink today, and I always liked sweet wine, but he poured me out a big water glass full. We hadn't had dinner, so I drank it down on an empty stomach.

By the time we got a mile and a half down the road, with these cattle, things were beginning to look blurry. We was supposed to count the cattle into the pasture, and I told Lloyd, "I can't count these cattle. Can you?" He said, "Yeah," so I drove them through the gate. When we get done, I asked him how many there was, and all he said was, "A hell of a lot of cattle!" He couldn't count them either.

When I got home, the wine really hit me. I got off to open the gate, and God, I was just loop-legged, all bundled up in chaps and a slicker, staggering up to the barn. Charles, who was three or four years old, come running out of the house and said, "Daddy, there's a preacher in the house!" Sure enough, the preacher had come out for services at the schoolhouse, and had stopped by to visit. I didn't want to go in there, probably taking four or five steps to get through the door, but I couldn't get back on my horse, either, so I stayed out there in the barn drunker than the devil, until the preacher left.

Our kids learned a lot at the Bar 13. The first winter or two, Charles didn't see anything but bulls, but then when I went to calving, he got to see cows and calves and he liked the little calves. One time, I had a calf chill down, so I brought him into the house, and Charles was all excited about bringing this calf in. The calf laid down by the fire on a rug, and Charles was petting him and saying what a nice calf he was, when the calf warms up a little bit and begins to come to, and goes "Blaaah!" God almighty, Charles fell over backwards, and then took off at a run through the clothes closet from one bedroom to another. That calf scared him to death.

We bought a Shetland pony when Charles was three and Shirley was six. One day in the winter, we went to cut some ice so the bulls could drink. I was afoot, but Shirley was setting up there on her little saddle when her pony decided he was thirsty. He walked right up to the water hole, socked his head down, and because it was hard for him to reach the water, he dropped down on his knees to drink. I had only one cinch on Shirley's saddle, so the saddle tipped up, and Shirley went right over the pony's head into the ice water.

When she fell, that scared the pony, and he lit out a-running, and my saddle horse run off after him.

Shirley was wet and screaming, but it was only a little ways back to the house.

Charles would come out on the pony with me, too. He'd help me feed the bulls and imagine he was driving cattle. He had a big black hat he found in the dump, and it would hang down over his eyes. One chilly evening, we was out together with the bulls, and Charles was riding along behind them whooping and hollering like a big cowboy, when all of a sudden the bulls started bucking and playing up. Charles' pony ran off, and Charles fell off on the ground. That scared him, and when I'd got the pony and put him back on, I had to lead the pony back to the house. Charles kept saying, "Daddy, don't turn this pony loose!"

That pony got so rollicky that in the end, I had to turn him over to some big kids until he was better broke to ride. He was a very good pony from there on out. Charles used to watch for me at night when I'd come in, and he'd have that pony up to wrangle some bulls, and we'd go out and talk about punching cows.

I left the Bar 13 in 1952, because I got too much responsibility. I had cattle in feedlots clear 'round the countryside, and cattle in the mountains, and they near about worked me to death. I never had a Sunday off, and I never could go to a school picnic with the kids. Fordyce was good to me, and I was young and active, and could handle a lot of work, but I got tired of it. So I gave them six months notice.

CHAPTER ELEVEN

SOME TALK ABOUT BREAKING HORSES

I've broke a lot of horses to work and to ride. My dad broke horses, and I worked around with him and picked it up and liked it.

The way I halter break colts that have been weaned is to catch them, put a halter on them, and pull them around to take some of the fight out of them. Then, you can tie them to a post, let them pull, and they will generally halter break themselves. When you lead them around after that, they'll try to jerk away from you, but you can handle them. I work with them like that for a day or two, turning them loose at night with the halter rope dragging on the ground, and catching them again every day to pull them around a little more. By then, they'll be pretty near halter broke.

It's different with older horses. In the olden days, fellers would rope a green horse and drag him out behind another horse and tie him onto a log. They'd leave him there night and day. He'd have grass to eat, and they'd water him maybe once a day, and by about the third day of being on a stake rope like that, a horse will lead, but he probably ain't gentled down too much.

A horse that's on a stake rope wears a hackamore, so he learns there is something around his head. He comes up against it until he figures out he has to turn. You tie him to something with a little give to it—it can be a log, or an old tire, or anything that will move. Something solid, like a post, brings him to such a quick stop that it can turn him right around and break his neck. Horses can actually drag a tire, if they take a hard run on it, but they can't get clear away. Pretty soon they'll turn around and face the tire. That helps when you go to riding them, because when you ride with a hackamore, or even a snaffle, they are used to the pull on their heads. They'll think about the times they hit the tire too hard, so when you put pressure on their heads, they've learned that they are supposed to come a little one way or another.

Once they learn to face a rope, they can start getting used to having one around their feet. They'll finally figure out a way to keep it out from under their feet, and if you leave it on long enough, they'll learn to step over it and pay no attention to it.

When a horse has never been on a stake rope, I use a big, braided nylon rope. It's flat and soft so it won't burn them, because a horse can hook a hind foot over that stake rope, back into it, and then go to kicking. A hard rope can burn him right down against the hoof and make him lame. A big, flat rope won't do that.

If you keep a horse on a rope three days, he's pretty well stake broke, and he will never forget that all his life. It worries them when they are haltered up with that rope around them. But, they teach themselves to get out of predicaments, and they learn to give with their head and learn to come up on a rope. It teaches them to lead.

People don't put a horse on a stake rope much any more because they think he'll get hurt. Horses have been hurt, although I never hurt one. I knew a fellow, though, that accidentally got a horse tangled up someway and broke his leg. It's like a person who's out walking and falls down and breaks a leg. You have to hit it just right for that to happen, and it don't happen very often.

You can take a horse that's cinchy or humpy and wants to buck, and tie him on behind a pickup, and start kind of easy, and keep going faster and faster, and pretty soon he gets to loping behind the pickup. If you've got him tied on solid, he's got to lope.

Of course, if a horse went to bucking and run out on that rope, you'd turn him over. A friend of mine, Greg Penson, broke a horse's neck that way, but he said, "Well, I'd rather break a horse's neck than a man's neck." If you're careful, though, and the horse has been led behind a pickup before, there's not too much danger, and you can learn an ornery horse to lead that way.

In the old days, once you had got a horse in and hung him on a stake rope for two or three days, you'd saddle him up, get on and go, and most likely take a lot of abuse up there on top. Nowadays, you work them in a corral first. You get them used to the saddle, and drive them, and get them so you can turn them, and so that they more or less know what to do.

A bronc stomper might tie up a horse's hind foot so he could get a saddle on him, and then he'd wool that horse around, get in and out of the saddle a couple of times, and then let the horse's foot down and ride. Sometimes them horses would buck, but they wore down. Of course, a young guy that's a bronc stomper, riding with a bridle or a hackamore, could reach up and pull the horse's head right around to his stirrup, and then step on him, and hit the saddle, and take him for a ride. If they are young and stout, they can get pretty tough on a horse.

Some fellers tie the horse's head around to the left, because that's the side you get on. If a young horse swings away from you when you're getting on, he can throw you and get away. But if a horse swings toward you, it throws you into the saddle.

The horse has all four feet free on the ground when he's on the stake, and then when you bring him into the corral for the first saddling, you tie up a hind foot and take a blanket up to him. You let the horse get the smell of the blanket, and then flip him over the ribs and back with the blanket, and finally get the saddle on him.

If a horse is real spooky, and you can't get up to him, I put on four-way hobbles. A four-way hobble is buckled around the front feet and the hind feet. There's a big ring in the middle, and a chain goes from the big ring to each foot, so the horse can about stand natural. The hobbles keep jerking him down until he finds out he can't go nowhere and can't kick you either. Then you, can pet him down the hind leg. The hobbles won't really upset a horse, unless they get tangled up somehow.

You tie up a hind foot so the horse can't jump out from under a saddle, and also so he can't kick you. You take a long rope, loop it around the horse's neck, so that it comes back against his shoulders like a collar, and tie a bowline knot that won't slip. Then, you get behind the horse and let the rope drag on the ground. The horse is going to jump back and forth until finally you get that rope between his legs. Some horses start kicking, but if they've been on a stake rope, they'll have got part of that out of them.

When I've got the rope between their legs, I walk up alongside the horse's shoulder where the loop comes back, and run the long end of the rope through the loop and pull on it. You got leverage enough to pull one hind foot up a little. He's going to fight some, but you can hold the rope in your hand. Pretty soon he will give up fighting, and then you take another wrap around his foot

Saddling the blue colt.

and go back through the loop and out again. Now, you got a double rope and you're holding the long end, so you take the rope back down and throw a half hitch over both ropes on the ankle, and that holds it on there.

If a horse ain't very bad, you don't have to get the hind leg off the ground very far, but, if he figures he is going to raise the devil and fight and kick, I'll tie his leg half way between the ground and his belly, so he can't get his foot to the ground at all. He's just standing on three legs, so there is no way he can kick you.

Colt with foot tied up during lesson with slicker. The horse had reared back and fallen to a sitting position.

Now you can throw your saddle on, and cinch it up, and let him get used to that. Then, I let him move around the corral with that foot up and let him wear down a little.

If a horse won't quick bucking under a saddle, I generally put a set of running Ws on him. A W is a set of ropes that goes from a strap around one ankle, up through a cinch ring under the belly, and back down to a strap on the other ankle, and back up through the ring, and you hold the long end. That way, when the horse starts to buck, you holler, "whoa," and stumble him. Sometimes, you throw him clear down. You can't help it if they tangle up, but after a little bit, they find out that they can't buck with a saddle. People say a W is cruel, but if you use them right, they're not. You don't set down on a W rope and jerk the horse's feet clear out from under him. You just pull him enough, 'til it kind of starts him down, and then you give him slack. That's what I call "stumbling" him.

There are knee pads you can put on a horse to keep from skinning their knees, and that's not a bad idea, because you can skin a horse's knees if he fights you too much. But, if you just stumble them—start them down and then give them slack so they get their feet back under them—pretty soon they find out they can't do nothing but stumble. Sometimes when you stumble them, they may hit their teeth on the ground. You really should have a soft corral. I don't have a soft corral, but I don't hurt a horse, because I don't throw him that hard. But, if you put weight on your rope, and they rear back, you can turn a horse clear flip-flop.

Ws are supposed to be bad, but it's the man using them that's wrong with Ws.

I always bit a horse even if I am going to ride him in a hackamore. I let him pack the bit in his mouth so he gets used to it. I put a snaffle bit on him and let him walk around the corral without any reins on. I let him just chew, and after he gets used to that, I put a rein on each side and tie it back to the saddle, generally to the cinch. I tie it kind of loose so he can walk and feel a little tension. Then, each day I tie him back a little more, 'til he gets used to the bit and walks with his head tucked. He finds that if he rams against the bit, it hits his mouth, and he also finds he can't throw his head up in the air.

After you keep them bitted long enough, and tied that way, it makes a horse walk with his head kind of tucked. There's a place up there in the poll they have to bend, and after a while it gets so that reflex is easy. Later, when you're riding and pull up on the reins, a horse will tuck his head and even learn to back up. He'll duck his head and then take a few steps backwards to stay away from the pressure of the bit.

Sometimes, when I'm bitting a horse, I'll tie his head around so they can't go but one way. That learns horses to go around in a circle. They can fight and put their heads over, and get mad, but finally their neck kinks, and they find it's easier to go the way you've tied them. Then, you tie them the other way. You don't have them over fifteen or twenty minutes tied one way or another, so their neck don't get to hurting too bad, but that really learns a horse to go.

That is what is called bitting a horse. It can take about three days and maybe more on some horses, but, by degrees, you make them bridle-wise. So you see, horses can learn a lot by themselves in the corral that you don't have to teach on top of them.

After a horse has been bitted, I put long driving reins on with a hackamore and work them in a corral. When you put the lines on them, you run them from the hackamore right through the stirrup. If you pull on the right line, that swings a horse to the right, and pulling on the left line swings him to the left. So a horse turns whichever way the pressure is. He learns to come around. I drive my horses on the outside, too. I put them ahead of a saddle horse and drive them outside the corral. That gets them used to a horse behind them, and you can still pull them one way and another, and turn them.

If you drive them around and around in a corral too long, a horse can get mad. If you quit just before he gets mad, then he has learned something. But, you can sull a horse sometimes by going on too long. He will stand there, and he won't give one way or another, and you can whip him, but he'll be so sour he will just stand there. After he does it once and gets away with it, he gets mad the next time and won't work for you. You can tell by how he is driving. If a horse is driving good, you can go ahead and drive him longer. But if he is not, why it's better to quit. After thinking about it overnight, he generally drives better. And every day it gets better, because he has learned more about being guided, and he don't get mad so quick.

When a horse is driving good, you can start riding him in a corral. I've got enough feeling in my hands about the way a horse is going to tell if he will handle a little when you get on top of him. Of course, when you get on a horse for the first time, he'll look back up and see something on top of him. That's what causes a lot of horses to buck. They are scared. They look up there, and here's a tall object up on top of them. That's where getting on and off comes in, when you've got one of their feet tied up, and they can't buck very much. A horse can jump a little, but he can't break loose and buck. And if you are young and active, and a horse gets to hopping around too much, and you're afraid he is going to fall down, you can jump out of the saddle and hit the ground.

Driving colt with long reins from another horse.

When I start to ride them, I'll take horses outside the corral, too, like when I'm driving them. Horses get madder in a corral than on the outside, because when you get one outside, and start him to going, he sees new country, and he's traveling, and different things keep his attention, and away he goes. In a corral, you just go 'round and 'round. I've seen horses guys was afraid to take outside, so they just rode them in the corral. After a while, them horses got what you called "corral sour." They'd just stand there. By God, you couldn't do nothing with them. After anybody's rode enough horses, you can tell when a horse is kind of loosened up, and you can take him right outside and go with him.

Just when a horse is ready to go outside is something that you've got to learn from the ground up. A set of reins is like a steering wheel on a car, or a tractor, or Cat with hand clutches. You've got to learn the feel of it. You get an idea from the feel of a horse's head that you can steer him one way and then another. When it's time to go outside, and when you can handle him, is something nobody can tell you. It's hard for a green boy that hasn't got the feel of that horse, but that's the row they got to hoe and learn it the hard way.

To start a horse neck reining, you take the reins in your right hand—if you are right-handed—and put the reins through your fingers, so that you can make the one or the other just a little bit tighter, while laying the other just a little on the horse's neck. To rein the horse to the right, you turn your hand to pull that right rein just a little bit tighter, but the horse also feels the left rein on the side of his neck. That's something that takes a little time, but pretty soon a horse goes to neck reining. Some pick it up a lot quicker than others, and you have to be careful in starting a horse to neck rein. If you use reins too much when horses are green, they start throwing their head. You are going to the right, and they throw their head to the left, 'cause they haven't learned to bring their head even. So, you shorten the rein—to keep their head kind of level.

That's some of the ways to start a horse. You have to figure a horse out and do different things with different horses. Some horses will do one thing good. Some will do everything wrong. They are like people.

CHAPTER TWELVE

THE FIFTIES

I went to work for Waldo Forbes at the Beckton Stock Farm in August, 1952. I had worked with Herefords and Shorthorns, but Waldo was breeding up Red Angus. He'd started about seven years before, buying up any registered Black Angus he could find that had thrown a red calf. He got them from all over the United States, and the first bull calf that he got come up from Florida in a crate.

My job was to look after the red cows and keep track of them. I had to keep the breeding book up to date, so you could tell from the ear tags and tattoos which calf came from which cow, and who the sire was. That's how registered outfits keep the blood lines straight.

One of the big events of my three years at Beckton, was the blizzard of '55. April 1 that year was a real nice day. It was a Saturday and the sun had been shining, though they predicted snow showers later on. Swede Teague was working at the stock farm with me, and we was out looking the calves over. Most of the calves were already on the ground, and we had the young ones and their mothers in an old sheep shed all strawed down. We rode home and dehorned some yearlings that day, and then Swede hitched a ride with somebody into town.

By midnight, it was snowing, and by daylight it was a howling blizzard. Swede tried to get back out by taxi—he'd got drunked up and called this woman taxi driver to

Sarah Holmes in later life, riding side saddle.

deliver him home—but they couldn't get through the storm.

In the morning, there was a lot of calves and cows standing in bunches because the natural protection wasn't very good. At the calving shed, the snow was drifting over the top and filling it up. I rode home, and then went back out in the afternoon, and by then it was all I could do to get up to the shed at all. We'd put poles across the front to keep the cows and calves from getting out, but with the snow piling up inside, they jumped out over the poles, and twenty-five or thirty of them were outside by then.

It had started as a wet snow, but then it turned freezing. The little calves' ears were so heavy with ice that they couldn't lift their heads up to suck, even if they could get to their mothers. That was all Sunday and by Monday morning the calves were in terrible shape.

An old sheep wagon set outside the shed, and another feller and I took ten gallons of warm milk up there, built a fire inside, and started grabbing calves and throwing them in the wagon, 'til they warmed up on the milk and the ice broke off their ears. Then, we'd put them back out again, but at least they was dry and had some nourishment. We saved a lot of calves that way.

The storm broke on Tuesday morning, and we rode out to see how things were. There were 250 calves on the ground and bunches of cows here and there, and the calves didn't know their mothers and the other way 'round. They can lose track of each other for good when they get snow and stuff rubbed on them, and they've rubbed up against other cattle, and the cows lose the scent of their calves. That's when you get "bummed" calves—calves whose mothers won't take them any more.

Luckily, these was registered cattle with numbers on them, so I could look them up and know which one belonged to which cow. The next day, I rode out and found all the registered cows with tight bags, and brought them to the barn, and locked them up in box stalls, and got them straightened out. We even got most of the grade cows and calves—the ones without numbers—straightened out when they went to milling together in the feed ground. I stayed out ahorseback all the time, helping them mother up, and in the end we come out of it real good. There was just one or two that we never got back on the mothers right.

Pauline won three dollars writing a story for the Sheridan Press about Ada, the Ayrshire, that disappeared in the blizzard. Ada was a big registered Ayrshire that was heavy with calf. If wasn't 'til three days after the storm that I saw this cow's head sticking out through the snow covering the flat cellar door of one of the little ranch buildings. The door lay flat above some steps that goes down into the cellar, and it must have been open, so Ada went on down, and the door blew shut and drifted over. Another door at the bottom of the steps went into the cellar itself, so Ada had just knocked it open and gone right in. She raised cain with cans and jars of stuff that were in there, but there was a little hay down there, too.

If she hadn't come back up the steps and stuck her head out, I doubt we'd have found her alive, but we got her all dug out, and she was thirsty, but okay. She went and got a big drink of water and wasn't any worse for wear. She never did have her calf, though. She fell and wrecked her leg, so she couldn't get up, and they shot her and tried to save the calf, but the calf died, too.

One summer night, we went to feed thirty bulls we had in, and we come up one short. We couldn't find him anywhere. I looked in a kind of culvert they'd sunk in the ground for a well. There was no water in it any more, and there was that bull, dead, sitting straight up on his tail. My guess is he'd been wrestling the other bulls and backed in, and then he hadn't been able to breathe right. He was a yearling about six feet long, and the culvert was ten feet deep, so it was three or four feet down to him. He was in the hot sun, with his head laid over to the side, smelling real bad. I put a top over the culvert, and we told Waldo Forbes what had happened. It was a Red Angus bull, probably worth $600 or $700 at that time.

Well, Waldo told his assistant manager to go get the tattoo number off that bull. I'd said I couldn't read it. So, this guy come down with his coveralls and a flashlight, because sometimes when you put a flashlight behind the ear you can see the tattoo more easily. I went with him and jerked the lid off that outfit, and he stuck his head down to read the tattoo and about fainted. He didn't have a very stout stomach, and I knew I wasn't going down into that mess with that stinking bull in that tight place. So, I suggested we run every bull through the chute and check all their tattoes, and the one we come up short—that's your bull. And that's what we done.

There was a big cookhouse at the Beckton Stock Farm with a porch upstairs and a balcony all the way around. Inside there was a kitchen, dining room, two bedrooms and lot of antique furniture. There was also a room with saddles and Navaho blankets in it. At one time in the earlier years, it was the house where the Forbes family lived. That cookhouse had a Chinese-laundry stove in the basement, a coal-fired water heater with a couple of lids on top. It didn't burn very well, so there wasn't much hot water for the dishes.

One afternoon in March, a kid named Rich Torrence and I was coming down from the calving shed, a mile away, when we seen the awfullest smoke rolling out all over. We thought the cookhouse was on fire. It must have been about three in the afternoon when we got over there. The cook's helper told us they'd just got the old heater burning, and that was where the smoke was coming from. I remember he said, "We're going to have hot water!" So, we drank a cup of coffee and worked around the barn some before going home.

Right after eight o'clock, Rich Torrence comes running in and says the cookhouse is on fire for real. I looked out the bedroom window and sure enough, I could see the flames. The old chimney was getting bad and the cement had cracked out of it, so there was a soot fire in the chimney that caught some of the siding they used to oil to make it look old.

They called the fire engine, but it ran off the road on the way out of town. It was a real cold night, too, and pretty soon after they got to the cookhouse, the fire hose froze shut. There was burning shingles flying around, starting fires down by the sheep barns, and some landing on our roof. I got out what hose we had at the house, but it froze too, and we couldn't get the water going. We were lucky the house didn't catch. Charles, who was nine, stood at the window and watched the fire late into the night.

The cook's helper, Benny, who'd been living in the cookhouse, stayed with us that night, and in the morning he realized his lower false teeth were in a cup up at the cookhouse, so his teeth was lost in the fire along with the furniture and the Navajo rugs.

Charles still had his pony when we were at the Beckton. He'd go play Indians with Rich Torrence's sister. She had a horse, and Charles would ride his pony with a rope in its mouth like the Indians did, and he'd be painted up like an Indian. I helped him start breaking ponies, too, and then he got a good cow horse we called Hopalong, because he'd kind of raise up and hop when he'd walk. Hopalong was a big-headed old roan horse that could really see a cow. Charles didn't use his pony much after that. He kept on going with horses, and working with me.

During our time at Beckton, my kids got into 4H Club work. I didn't pay much attention to it until I started fitting show cattle, and then the kids was getting older, and 4H had the same kind of program. Shirley started in the sewing program about 1952, but then she went to the fair, and saw other kids taking care of their steers, so she wanted one, too. She must have been ten or eleven when we got her first little Hereford steer. It was a Comprest steer, which was the kind they were showing then, and she called him T-Bone.

The next year, Charles was old enough to get in. You was supposed to have only one steer in your project, but I bought two for Charles the first year, and another for Shirley, so they was feeding four steers for quite a while. Shirley quit 4H about '58, and Charles went on 'til about '61, working with a horse. Horses is a big deal now in the 4H, but back then there wasn't prize money for horses. They'd just ride out a horse or two, and they didn't even show much at halter.

Doing their own work—that's what was important for the kids. Mine said if it hadn't been for 4H, it would have been a lot harder for them to get around. Charles said it meant a lot to him when he went to wrangling dudes at Teepee Lodge. He'd never been away from home, or worked a crew of men before, but because of his time with 4H around people he did okay. He was going to be a 4H leader the last year he was here, and that was what he was trying to get across.

I remember three horses in particular from the Beckton: Jailbreak, Breeze and Loki. Jailbreak was a stud out of a registered quarter-horse stud and a thoroughbred mare. I always liked that cross. It slows them down a little bit and gives them a little more sense, and it really makes nice horses. Jailbreak was a big, powerful brown horse with a blaze face, and he had real cow sense. He was gentle, but if he decided he didn't want to do something, he wouldn't do it. I started breaking him to ride one fall after the breeding season, when he was six or seven years old.

One of the things he didn't want to do was take the lead. He was used to being rode in the middle of a bunch of horses. I kind of gig a horse along and generally ride in the lead. There is fellows ride faster than I do now, but I've always got a saddle horse in the lead of everybody else. I'm kind of hard on people that ride with me. So, I had a lot of work to do with Jailbreak, and I beat and pounded and spurred on him until I thought I had him going pretty good.

Well, he turned out to be the horse that crippled me. Four of us was out riding one day—Swede Teague, Charlie McCormick and somebody else—and I was trying to ride in the lead, because we was on a narrow trail going out on Powder River where you've got to ride single file. I got off and got a cottonwood club to bat Jailbreak on the neck with, to keep him headed out. It was just a round stick, and I'd pop him with it, and it sounded worse wicked than it was. We headed down this steep bank, and Jailbreak whirled right around. It was slick, frozen gumbo, and his feet flew out from under him, and he slid to the bottom. I got away from him, but I slipped a disc in my back. I was hurting bad, and Charlie McCormack said, "For Christ's sake don't die. It's too hard digging!"

For a long time, they didn't know it was a disc. I got X-rayed and they couldn't find anything wrong, and I took some chiropractic treatments that near about killed me. It hurt so bad I would go into the bar and have a double shot and then get in the car to drive home, and I'd lay one leg over to the side and feed the gas with the other foot, because the one was all numb. The pain went right down my leg. I can see how anybody can be an alcoholic from pain.

Finally, a doctor said he thought it was a slipped disc. He told me to go over to the Capitol Drug Store and get myself a corset with all them stays, and that started bringing me a little relief. I rode with that thing on for two years, and for a long time I was stiff as a board, bracing myself with my hand against the saddle horn, because I didn't want to take any jar on my back. It took two years, but it finally wore itself out, and I'm glad it did.

Breeze was a daughter of Jailbreak's, and she was the smartest cow horse I ever rode. She was just halter broke when I found her with twenty foot of smooth wire caught around her hind leg. She had a bad burn from that wire, and she couldn't travel, but she wouldn't let me cut it off with the pliers I carry on my saddle. So, I nipped off enough of it so she could walk, and then I led her in to the ranch to where I could get the rest off.

I kept an eye on her and doctored her, and she never did go lame from that wire. When she healed up, I broke her to ride, but I had an awful time doing it. She didn't buck, but she'd see something and get spooked, and then want to balk and rear up to go back to the barn. I started to carry a gunny sack, and when she spooked, I'd jerk the sack out and wave it. That would scare her, and she'd forget about going back.

She was a booger. I was going down the highway early one morning to brand, and she was a fast-running walker, and we was really clipping it off, when a lady came by in a car just as we was passing a highway sign. That lady hooted the horn and my God, Breeze fell back through herself. Every time she saw a highway sign after that she'd rear up and run backwards.

But, when I got her with cows, she really went to work. The last night I rode her, I turned her into a pasture for a day off. There was some cows in there that I'd been putting in the barn every day with her, and when I turned her loose, she started after one of the cows all by herself 'til she drove that cow right into the barn. The next day, she got into a cattle guard and hurt her ankle, and I never rode her again. One day she fell on that weak ankle, broke her leg, and that was the end of that. She was a really smart horse. I wished I could have owned her.

Loki was a thoroughbred. I rode him a jillion miles, and he was a real nice horse to ride. He was hot and nervous, but I got along with him and could do anything with him. With Loki, you never rode behind a bunch of horses. You had to be in the lead.

He would hardly ever stand still, but he seemed to know when my back was hurting. I could lead him out to a bale of hay, and he'd stand there as quiet as can be, while I'd get up on it and get on him. But when I'd be "at myself," feeling good, why he'd be a-prancing.

There are many ways to move cows. One time at the Beckton, when we were weaning calves, there was this black cow with a big calf sucking on her, and she was stifled. That means she was hurt in the stifle joint in the hind leg, and she was awfully lame. We started gathering the cattle down by a reservoir where there was some muddy, boggy ground, and somebody turned this old black cow away from getting into the reservoir. Well, she got down into that swampy ground, and bailed off a four-foot bank into the mud to where she was right up to her sides and couldn't get out.

Rich Torrence was there, and he knew how to run a Cat. So, he gets the Cat, and we hooks a rope on that cow and pulls her down through that mud onto dry ground. After that, we went on with the others—forty or fifty head in that bunch—and drove them on in to wean the calves off, and the black cow's calf went along, too.

I rode back the next day to see if the black cow had fallen back into the mud hole, but she was gone. I found her back over a hill in a big brush patch. It was all thick thorns and cherries and stuff, and I left her there.

Swede Teague was working at the Beckton then, so he and I went back up to the brush patch to get that cow. We got off our horses and worked her up to the edge on foot, figuring we might be able to get her out in the open and drive her. All at once, she turns right back over the top of us, and we couldn't stop her. She got to where it was a little open, and we managed to hang a loop on her and thought we'd hold her with the rope, and snub her, and get her out in the open—but she laid down. She was so poor and crippled there was nothing we could do with her. We had to turn her loose and go home.

One Saturday afternoon, I saddled up to ride out in the hills. Swede asked me where I was going, and I told him, "I'm going to get that old black cow." He said, "A fifth of whiskey says you'll never do it."

I rode up to where that old cow was, still in the brush. So, I got off and hobbled my horse, and set in the shade, and smoked a cigarette. That old cow looked at me—and looked at me some more—and then hopped into the brush aways. I didn't holler or anything. I just moved up a little closer. I set there until she went a little ways further, and then I moved up some more. She was getting nervous about me not hollering or trying to make her do anything. She got up to where she'd turned back on us the last time, and I figured she'd come over me again, but I just kept quiet and set there. She looked at me, and then she walked out of the brush, just a little bit.

Finally, she decided she didn't want to be in the brush patch with me, so she starts hopping over the hill across a half mile of open country toward the reservoir. I went and got my horse, taking my time, because that cow was really lame. Once we were out in flat country, I heaved a rope on her because I figured, by God, if she got ornery I could get her through a gate into a field, and we'd be able to come get her with a horse trailer.

I didn't tighten the rope much. The cow kind of steered around through a gate that went into a field that led to the main road back to the barn. It was a mile and a half. Once she got through the gate, I let her go. When she hit the road, she knowed where she was going, and so she went a-hopping right into the barn. Swede was standing in these big, wide doors, leaning on them, and here come this old cow up the road trailing a rope. He said, "You do the damndest things to make a liar out of somebody!" I told him I went up there and just set, and that got her confused.

Anyway, it was worth a fifth of whiskey to me.

The assistant manager at the Beckton was a very good guy in a lot of ways, but he wasn't really a ranch man. I don't want to use his name here, so I'll call him Brett. He'd believe just about anything we told him, so, of course, we pulled pranks on him.

Brett couldn't tell one horse from another—even his own. He used to ride a saddle horse called Dewey, and one day he walked into the barn when somebody had Dewey in there shoeing him. "What horse is that?" Brett asks. The guy answered, "This damn outfit makes me so mad keeping all these old horses that's only fit for the canner. This one ain't worth a dime!" Brett was always making notes, so he says, "I'll make a note of that and tell Mr. Forbes to sell that horse." Of course, then the guy told him it was Dewey.

Brett had a weak stomach. One time, we was camped up in the mountains at a holding pasture. There was Brett and me, our two boys and a kid from the ranch. That night, we got to talking about burning cow chips, and after dark the kids had a big time getting cow chips and putting them on the flames.

The next morning, I got up and started making breakfast by the lights of the pickup. It's blowing real hard, but I get some eggs and bacon made when Brett comes up and looks at the fried eggs, and says, "My God, Ray, you got too much pepper on them this morning. I can't eat them." "Pepper hell," I said, "that's them cow chips blowing around." "Oh my God," he said, and he set his plate down on a rock. Of course, it *was* pepper, but breakfast was over for him.

Another time, he came into the cookhouse on a winter morning to have a cup of coffee and talk about the day's work like he'd do every morning. Well, in winter, when it got real cold, sometimes the water would freeze up and there wouldn't be any coffee water. It was real cold that day, and when the cook poured him some coffee, Brett said, "I didn't think you'd have water this morning." The cook said, "Well, one of the fellers took a bath last night and forgot to drain the bathtub, so I used that." "Oh my God," said Brett, and he set his coffee down and never touched it again. That's the way it always was in bunkhouses and cookhouses when someone was a little green.

After I left Beckton, I was on a different ranch each year for the next three years. I went to the Cross H the first of June in 1955 and left in September. The manager and I never hit it off from the word go. He didn't know much about handling cattle.

From there, we went to the NX east of Sheridan for the winter. It was owned by the Bar 13 people, but had a different brand. Swede Teague was there, too. We weaned calves, and did the fall work, and four of us dehorned 400 head of cows. We'd go gather a bunch of cows and wean the calves off, work out the horned cows and leave them in the corral overnight, and then we'd be out there at daylight and go to sawing off horns. One guy ran the chute and the three others rotated so that two was sawing all the time. We figured we could dehorn one cow a minute, and when we got done, we had a pile of horns that looked like a haystack.

That winter of '55 was really cold. We trailed 400 head of cattle from Badger Creek to Sheridan one time when it was twenty below zero, and the snow was deep, and the wind was blowing. I wrapped my boots in newspaper before slipping them into overshoes. That makes good insulation. And I put on my chaps and all the clothes I'd got. But, one young fellow along that didn't have no buckles on his overshoes, and he wasn't dressed too heavy, and he near about froze to death.

Jack Reisch, who managed the NX, went into town and got a fifth of whiskey, and Allen Fordyce brought out some lunch and another fifth, and I'd never seen him do that before. There was only two of us—me and a fellow called Bob Miller—who was drinking, so we drank plenty of whiskey.

We had to trail right through the town of Big Horn, and on the way through, one of them yearlings took off up a side street that was all ice. Well, Bob Miller just under-and-overed his horse across the ice and brought that steer back. He was riding a barefooted horse, that means his horse didn't have no shoes, and he'd never have done it if he hadn't been a little drunked up. But he came back with that steer and said, "Well, I guess I turned that son of a gun!"

So, I spent that winter rawhiding and driving cattle, and then in the spring of '56, I went up to the Hidden Valley ranch, a registered outfit of about 150 cows. I thought it was going to be a good job, but it didn't turn out that way.

The Hidden Valley was a very small place with not more than 700 acres of deeded land and a little more that was leased. When you work on a little outfit like that, you do everything from brushing cattle to putting up hay, and like I said, I thought we'd have a pretty good deal. But, it wasn't part of the deal for me to mow lawns, and when I got stuck with lawn mowing it made me mad. I might have mowed a little lawn, but at Hidden Valley, I'd have to go over and mow the big house yard. The owner's wife would look out the window and say, "Trim this up a little," and I rebel when it comes to getting down on your prayer bones and crawling around to work in a damned flower bed. They'd have a big party once in a while, and you were supposed to go over there and stand around in a coat and park cars. I wouldn't do that. The hell with it. God damn, the bigwigs could park their own cars! So I left there in April of '57.

While I was at the Hidden Valley, my father died of cancer of the stomach. He'd been sick for about a year. He was always a big, husky man, but he started getting thin and didn't care to eat, and finally, he went to Gillette, and they found this big tumor. He didn't want it operated on, but my mother kept after him, so he came to Sheridan and Dr. Rhodes opened him up. But, there was no chance of taking the tumor out, and he only lived about two months after the operation. He never seemed to suffer much. He got weaker and weaker and starved to death, because he couldn't digest his food. He just went to sleep.

My mother moved into Hulett and spent the rest of her life there. It was just a few miles from where she was born.

The next place I worked was the Cedar Strip outfit, and that was only for a year. Joe Mates was leasing it, and we didn't get along too good. He'd told me if I worked a year he'd have a good house fixed up for me, and there'd be a bus into Hardin for the kids to go to school. By this time, Shirley was finishing high school, and Charles was still in grade school. But after I got out there, I seen the handwriting on the wall. There was no way Mates could put a house and electricity out there for us, because the owner wasn't going to spend all that money and put a house on a leased place. Saying that was just a way to get me up there to work.

I went out to the ranch as cattle foreman, and the family lived in Big Horn. There was supposedly 100,000 acres in the Cedar Strip, and after they took me through it once in a jeep, I was supposed to gather 1,500 head of cattle. It's really hard work to get into a strange country and figure out how to gather it. It was rough out there, and I had to work hard to learn it. We'd go out before dawn to gather one bunch of cattle, and then come in for some grub at ten-thirty or eleven in the morning, and then I'd saddle up a horse in the heat of the day and go ride to plan how I was going to place the men the next morning. I'd be double-riding that country because I didn't know it yet, and I had to be ahead of the men all the time. I done a lot of riding while the rest of the boys was lying in the shade!

We had trouble with cooks at the Cedar Strip outfit. The first one liked to get into the whiskey. Drinking could be a real problem in a bunkhouse, and I had them fellows at the ranch pretty well trained not to let me see them drinking. I found out after that Charles was making a quarter or fifty cents to sit by a window in the bunkhouse and watch to see when the old man was coming! But, that cook didn't last long.

So, I hired another and brought him out. At least, he said he was a cook. The first night everything was half burned up. Christ, I could cook that good myself, so when we got done eating, I loaded him up and hauled him back to Sheridan.

After that, I hired a man and wife, and she was a pretty good ranch cook, but he wasn't worth much. He was a great talker, telling what he could do, and all the while he was just getting by. When I got ornery with him, he got mad and quit, so that was another cook down the drain.

After that woman left, we put the men out in camps, and I boarded at headquarters with Tuffy Brown, the outfit's manager. Pauline and the kids was still in Big Horn. That winter, I rode to check on the men in the camps, and looked after the cattle, and it wasn't too bad a winter outside of being away from home.

Tuffy and I got along real good, but Joe Mates had it in for him. In the spring, Mates said to me, "You could do a lot more for this outfit if Tuffy wan't around here. He's holding you up." I said Tuffy was doing fine and that I didn't want the whole outfit. But, then Mates went off to Denver for a few days and left a letter on Tuffy's desk. It said he would have to be out by the first of April, and that I was going to move my family in and take charge of everything. Tuffy said, "Why that yellow son of a gun not telling me to my face. And he even wrote it on yellow paper!"

We didn't have a phone out there at the ranch, so Tuffy and I goes into Hardin and to call Denver. Tuffy says, "Mates, are you going to have a man out here the first of April?" He says yeah, so Tuffy says, "Well if it ain't too much trouble, you better bring two." "What do you mean?" says Mates. So, I gets on the phone and says, "Yeah, just bring another man because I'm a-leaving, too." So, Tuffy and I both pulled out on the first of April and left him afoot.

CHAPTER THIRTEEN

SOME TALK ABOUT GEAR

You have what kind of equipment you can afford, but when you are riding all the time, you want your own saddle and your own gear, so you can do what you like with it. You get the kind of a saddle you like to ride, and you get the stirrups set your own way. The saddle you ride all the time, you don't loan much to anybody else, because the stirrups will not be quite the same if you keep changing them up and down. They don't get rode down to one position. If somebody else gets on your saddle, the left stirrup will always seem a little bit longer than the right, because you get on that side all the time. When you ride all the time, you just get used to that little difference, but somebody else will notice it.

Some of the old-time saddles that was long and narrow they called an A Fork. The first bronc-riding saddle was real deep, with a high back and high swells in the front. You set down deep. And there was a stock saddle that was deep with fourteen-inch swells, so your legs kind of set under the swells. Then, sometime around World War II, they began to make saddles flatter, with smaller swells on them, and a low cantle or back. Cantles used to set straight up, but nowadays they roll back, and it gives you a place to set in there. They call them roll cantles, and they're really nice because they don't hit you in the middle of the back. Some of them old cantles was six to eight inches high.

Then, they started making bronc-riding saddles for rodeos—Association saddles with a rounding swell on them, and the cantle not very high, but kind of rolled back a little bit. All saddles at rodeos are regulation Association saddles, so everybody rides the same tree. That gives everybody the same chance riding, because if they had different ways of building them, someone might have more leverage. Them first old bronc saddles must have had a fourteen- or fifteen-inch swell that run out kind of pointed. Riders could put their feet in the stirrups, and grip that saddle under the swells, and get a lot more leverage. The Association saddle is more rounding, so riders need more balance. Some of these young fellows still use deep saddles for riding a colt a time or two.

You've got to watch a bunch of horses in a corral with saddles on. There's always some horse that might take a bite out of one. That's happened to a lot of guys' saddles. They like the salt in the leather.

You should oil saddles at least once a year. That really helps where the sweat is. You use saddle soap, and clean them all up, and then put neats-foot oil on. That preserves the leather. Nowadays, they've got a saddle-soap and oil mix they call "New Look." You go over a saddle with that, and wipe it all off, and it puts some oil in the leather, plus it looks new and shiny. Neats-foot oil, on a new saddle, turns it black and takes the new look off.

I've had all kinds of pads and blankets. I never had a Navajo until fifteen or twenty years ago. I've only had two of them, and they was both given to me. I've had all kinds of blankets up to these latest ones that are white with air between the layers. They're real easy on a horse. I don't know what it is inside, it's not foam, but something like hair or sheepskin doubled up and sewed together so it leaves air space. It looks like muslin. It's the same stuff they use in hospitals to heal bed sores. It takes up the sweat pretty good and stays dry. A lot of people ride them just that way, but I put a Navajo on top. It makes a pretty good-looking outfit.

Guys that's roping need a double-rig saddle. Most of them ride full double-rigs in the arena, because that cinches the front end of the saddle down good, and the back cinch holds it down for jerking stock around.

Riding out here in the hills and doing ordinary roping, you don't need that full double. It puts the cinch up closer to the front legs and has a tendency to make sores on your horse. Fixing mine the way it is now pulls it back so I don't ring-sore my horse. And I ain't got the back cinch. With a double rig, you generally have a mohair cinch in front, and your back cinch is wide leather. With a full double-rig saddle cinched up to the front, if a horse jumps up in the air with you, that saddle can tip way up and the back cinch will hold it.

When you're harnessing a horse, there's a lot to fitting collars. To some guys, it doesn't make any difference: a collar is a collar. But, there's a lot in having a collar fit just right for width and length. For length, to give enough room, you get it so that you can about slip your hand under it easy. If it's too short, it'll make a horse's neck sore. It'll pinch him.

If a horse works with his head high, he needs a longer collar, and if he works with his head low, you put a shorter collar on, because it throws the draft down on the point of the shoulder. That's where the big end of the pull comes in, the flat place on the shoulder. If a horse works with his head down, that throws a lot of slack in the collar, and it makes him sore on the point of the shoulder. Collars run in all sizes, so you've got to hang your harness behind your horse and know what collar goes on each horse. Then you get your places marked and everything.

Poor-fitting collars cause awful sores on horses. I know a little bit about it. A lot I don't know, but I used to be able to keep my horses from getting sore shoulders.

A hackamore is a simple bridle without a bit you can start young horses with. It goes around the nose. You generally pull it up so it sits up towards their eyes and is low behind, so when you are riding along, there's no pressure on the horse's jaw at all. But, when you pull up on it, it squeezes up on the lower jaw. With the front high and low behind, it pulls down and tightens on the nose, so it works up and down like a lever.

Hackamores are good to ride young horses with 'til you get them going. You can ride a horse quite a while with a hackamore, 'til he gets smart. Some horses find they can throw their heads up, so then you've got to go to bitting them. But, I have rode horses a long time with a hackamore, and they handled just as well as they did with a bit.

You can pull sideways on a hackamore, and a horse won't fight like he will with a bit in his mouth hurting him. A snaffle will hurt the sides of the mouth, but it don't hurt the bars at the top of the mouth. With a hackamore, they don't have anything in their mouth to worry them, and you can pull them one way and another when they don't neck-rein. You can set down on a rein and swing a horse around without hurting his mouth. After he's rode with a hackamore, it don't take as long for him to get bitted. He knows more or less how to stop and turn around.

Ray Holmes on Snipper, using a hackamore, 1979.

There are one-eared bridles that go over only one ear of a horse, and there are bridles with browbands across the horse's forehead, and a band back behind his ears with a throat latch. They used to ride a lot of them that way, but nowadays they are kind of out of style.

A long time ago when I was riding, you put the ear bridles on tight, and you never had a throat latch on them. It's just a man's opinion, but I like these one-ear bridles now with the throat latch, because I don't have trouble with the horse rubbing them when you get off and tie him up. If you didn't have a throat latch, some of the old smart horses that you got off and on all day would rub, and get it started off down over an ear, and then they'd pull back and break your bridle. When you have a throat latch, it helps keep them on. I've had old smart horses you couldn't hardly tie up with a bridle. They'd just work it 'til they got loose.

There is a lot of difference in bridles and bits, and everybody has their own idea. I like a bit with a long shank that curves back on a horse so it will check him, but it don't hurt him. If a bit comes down with a fairly long shank that tips back, you don't get as much leverage on a horse as with a straight shank. It's an easy bit.

I don't have as many bits as a lot of guys. One bit I like has been welded up a lot, but it's got a copper port in it with a little cricket, or roller, in the middle which most horses like. If they're kind of nervous, they click that with their tongue. Copper makes a horse's mouth moist. When you ride a horse, and he gets hot, and his mouth gets dry, he has a tendency to get harder mouthed. Copper keeps the saliva coming. I like that little cricket, or roller, in there. You can hear a horse when he wiggles his tongue and clicks that little wheel, and it's not rough on him.

Whips have their purpose. I had a blacksnake—a bull whip, some call them—that works pretty good. Sometimes, if you get a cow or a bull that don't want to turn, you can hit them a few licks with that whip, and it will make them turn. And I use it a lot to drive calves crossing creeks and stuff. I don't hit the calves much, but hit behind them in the grass, and it scares them and makes them jump ditches. They hear a noise behind them and jump ahead. And there are rawhide whips that, if they are used right, are good for cutting out cattle in the corral. You don't have to whip them much, but maybe there's an old cow that's slow, and you can hit her, and she'll step up. Rawhide whips are especially good standing in a gate sorting cows and calves. You let a cow go by and the calf starts up, because he's not crowded too close behind, and you can snap the whip right in front of his face. You don't necessarily hit him, and he'll jump back and won't go by you. If you don't have anything like that, he may follow the cow. Or, you can touch him a little with it on his head, and it will stop him.

Just to get in a corral and go to whipping and slashing don't do any good, but there is times when some old cow won't come through the bunch, and you can kind of walk back, and turn around, and pop her with the whip, and she'll walk on out. They call them rawhide whips "stock whips," and they work all right, but so many times whips is overdone in a corral. If everybody's whipping and slashing, they don't do any good.

Clothing is something else that has changed a lot, particularly clothing for cold weather. For instance, you can buy down-filled jackets, and pants, and thermal underwear. It used to be just wool and cotton underwear and shirts, and chambray shirts that wasn't Western cut.

There was overalls and some wool pants. But now you can buy lined, insulated pants and footwear. They used to have sheepskin or felt shoes—heavy felt and leather. Now they have insulated overshoes and insulated cowboy boots. I've never had a pair, but those that do say they're awful warm. I've got some felt shoes that are good for keeping your feet warm. You can put a down sock on besides, and a few times when I went out with all that on plus overshoes, your feet's like you got them against the heating stove.

A few people nowadays still wear these insulated coveralls, which are really warm, but I never owned a pair. I've seen people ride in them, but they don't look like they was made for riding. They're all right in really subzero weather, but if it's warm they're too warm. I wear a light shirt—just a T-shirt—and then a heavy wool shirt, and then a wool jacket over that, and a coat—and that makes a lot of layers. It's light and it's warm.

They used to have old sheepskin coats that was so heavy they'd make your shoulders ache. I wore a lot of them. The sheepskin coats and wool mackinaws were so cold they would freeze you to death. Now they've got all these light, down-filled coats. Down is really something. If you've got the money nowadays, you can really dress warm.

I dress different now than I used to, I wear two pair of pants when it's cold, but I still put on old leather shotgun chaps. They really stop the wind, but I don't wear them except in the winter time. I've got tallow in mine, and when it gets cold, they're kind of stiff and make it hard to get on a horse. They used to be real soft and pliable, but they leaked. So, I took them out on a hot day and poured a lot of tallow on and let that soak in. That turns water over the knees.

Everybody used to ride pretty much with batwing chaps. They're made of leather and used to have different width wings on them—from a foot up to sixteen inches. Batwing chaps is big and wide. You get to riding in the wind, and them floppy wings'll blow out on your horse. You'd better be a young man because that'll spook your horse.

Nowadays, everybody uses shotgun chaps with zippers. They had shotgun chaps in the old days, but you had to step into them pretty near barefooted, because they had no buckles or zippers. Shotgun chaps are, you might say, like overalls with no seat. Then they made some that had three buckles you would buckle halfway down. Now they put zippers in them, and all you need to do is just lay the chap around you and zip them back down, so you can have your overshoes on when you put them on. They're warmer than a batwing chap, because they're tight when you zip them up.

And then, the young fellows wear chink chaps nowadays that keep your clothes clean. They come a little bit below the knee, and some fellows wear them with high-top boots. Chink chaps will keep you dry up to a point, but they're not like long chaps. They're more of a working chap, the way I see it. You can wear them branding and wrassling calves, and they keep your knees clean on the ground. I seen them first six or seven years ago, when men in chink chaps got to drifting in. Probably they was in Texas and Nevada and places like that before.

So there's batwings, and shotguns, and little old short chink chaps—something I didn't know about till just a year or two ago. They used to wear angora chaps made out of angora goat skins. They was warm in the winter, but if they got wet, God, they weighed a hundred pounds to the leg! So you don't see any of them anymore. Only in a museum.

Cold weather and brush—that's what chaps was made for. And you pronounce it with an sh- sound like *sheep*, not like *chapped* hands, the way some TV commercials do nowadays.

I've had many a pair of boots in my time, because I've never worn anything but boots for years. I bought a pair of shoes one time that was a little too small, and I give them away. And then, I had a pair of shoes that a friend gave me. They was an expensive pair of shoes, and they fit me, and once in a while I would put them on to do some fencing. Not very often. But I can't find them now, so I guess I gave them away, too.

You used to be able to get a pair of Blucher boots made to order for $25 that would now cost over $150. That was a good pair of boots. It's a lot easier to get boots made to order now than it used to be, because so many people just buy them out of the store. Not as many people have made-to-order boots.

All the boots I ever saw used to be high-heeled with about sixteen-inch tops. They still have high tops, but many now is made without a steel shank in them and with real flat heels. The little narrow stirrups they used to ride—ox bow and some of the others—took a high-heel boot with steel shank in them. They wasn't over an inch to an inch and a half wide. The stirrup fit right under the arch of your foot, and the high-heel boot kept your foot from going through, while the steel shank kept the stirrup from pushing up so hard on the bottom of your foot. Nowadays they use big, wide-bottom stirrups three and four inches wide, so they can wear soft boots. Even bronc riders wear a flat-heeled boot with a light sole. They claim they can grip the stirrup better.

The only place they use narrow stirrups now is when they ride broncs, but they split the boots so they'll come off real easy. They split the sides, so if they hang up, the boot will come off. Tight-fitting boots are hard to pull off. A horse can drag you, which can be fatal.

I can't keep my feet warm in winter unless I've got boot overshoes. Nowadays, they put a lining in. I don't wear any heavier socks in the winter time, but you want clean overshoes with that lining in them and a pair of loose boots. When they're new, overshoes are really warm. But after they get older, and they get damper and leak, they're pretty cold.

I guess I would wear store-bought boots, but I never got a pair that seemed to fit just right. They're a little too wide. Manybe I don't pay enough money for them.

I don't ride much with spurs. Spurs get a horse's attention and make him move quick, so if they are used right, why they are a good thing. But, I don't like to ride young horses with spurs, because you get to spurring them, and they get used to them spurs, and they get what you call "dead bellied." You can just spur on them, and they don't pay much attention. But, if you get a horse that has never been rode with spurs, and he gets lazy, and you use a pair of spurs on him and touch him, boy it wakes him up!

You can also hang up with spurs, and that's why they have changed the spurs for rodeo events nowadays. They're a little band spur of spring steel, I suppose, and you don't have a spur strap. They slip right on a boot, and there is a little rowel on them. If you were roping and jumped off a horse, if that little spur caught, it would slip off.

If you're out here riding in the hills, and your horse falls down, a spur can catch on the saddle or a back cinch. I had that happen once when the big rowelled spurs I used to ride went through and was under my back cinch. It was a little loose, and when I stepped off, the spur was into the back cinch, where you can't get your foot out. I had a good hold on the reins, and I stepped right back on my horse and jerked the spur out. I didn't get hurt.

Then last summer, I had a long rope strap that I should never have had. It was a strap I'd made in a hurry and split so it would go over the saddle horn. I had my rope down driving cows, and that split went right over the shank of my spur. You probably couldn't do that once in a thousand times. But, if a guy I was riding with hadn't told me, and if I had stepped off to open a gate, I would have come part way over and been hung up on the horse. I'd have got my foot about half on the side, and I'd have been hung. If the horse had jerked away from me, that spur would have never come out of there, and I might have got kicked and drug to death. So, that's about the last time I wore them big rowelled spurs and I cut the rope strap off. It don't take much of a strap to hold you, and it don't take long for a horse to kick you in the head.

Knock on wood, I've never had a bone broke or even been badly hurt, except for my back that time. I'd say the good Lord's had his hand on my shoulder.

When I was a young fellow growing up, everybody wore big, five-gallon, rolled-rim hats. I used to wear one, and it made my face look about as narrow as a hand. Then they quit roll-brims for a long time and put on straight brims, but not near as big. But, now they're coming back with some rolled-brim hats again: You'll see some of them around.

I like a straight brim. They wear them quite a lot bigger, and they're different because they kind of fit down all the way around. In my time, we rolled them up so a hat was pointed to the front.

To fix your hat, you can put a string that comes around the front of it, and poke two holes just back of your ears, and take the string around, and pull it up and tie it in the front of the hat. That makes a loop across the back of your head so the wind won't blow your hat off. Otherwise, if the wind catches it, it can go right past a horse's head, and that can cause you to get bucked off if it's a spooky horse. You usually have it pushed down pretty tight in front, so it won't blow off the other way.

There's all kinds of creases in hats—stockman's creases and all—I can't tell you all the creases they've got. There used to be an old-time crease I believe they called a Tom Mix. It was pointed right up to the top. And then they had a little hat with a not very big rim and kind of high-crowned they called a Congressman's hat. There's been all kinds. I haven't paid any attention to creases anymore. I used to know when I bought a hat what kind of crease it had. Mine is just kind of creased in down the middle and the back. I don't know what they call that.

At one time a few years back everybody used straw hats. They was awful looking, so wide and big. Then they started getting straw hats that looked like felt hats, and people went wild over them. There are still quite a few of them, but it's just a fad. But they are cooler than felt in the summer.

Caps have been around as long as I have. They used to have warm Scotch caps made of real heavy felt. And they had some little ear flaps, but you could also pull them right down over your ears without turning the flaps down. Everybody wore Scotch caps, and after a while they got old and pointed up like a sock, and they looked funny. The big end of people that work outside now wear caps instead of hats. Most everything is caps. But I always liked a hat. My ears sunburn with a cap on except late in the fall or early spring.

I guess the reason cowboys wore big hats was they kept the sun off, and you could also curl them up and get a drink of water. And the brim protected their eyes from the sun, and when you dipped your head down and looked at the ground, them brims would keep dirt and snow from blowing in your eyes.

When I get to talking, I'm always a-tipping my hat from one side to the other. That's a force of habit. Not everybody does that, but I have noticed other guys do it, too. It's just a habit. Sometimes I push a hat back, or I tip it this way, setting around and talking. I'm always changing my hat. It's nervousness, I guess, and you can pull your hat down and look down if you don't want to see somebody.

You generally can tell pretty much about a cowboy by his clothes. You can be fooled up to a point, but not too far. If a guy's not used to wearing cowboy clothes, you can tell the first outfit he gets by the way he gets around and sets his hat on the head. And you can tell by the way a greenhorn walks on a new pair of boots that he's never walked on boots before. Of course, now they're getting so many flat-heeled boots that they can buy a pair of boots like shoes, but then some of these men's shoes is getting so high-heeled that they look ridiculous, way up there like that.

Cowboy style is sure changing. In the early days, guys had whiskers and long hair, but that's because they couldn't get to a barber. When they'd get into town, they'd kind of shave and clean up. Then, in my time, it was just a few of the older guys that wore moustaches, and then everybody went clean-shaved. Nowadays, you go to a rodeo and there's lots of them wearing their hair and whiskers long.

So time changes a lot of things. I never was a fancy dresser or anything like that, but when I was a young feller, I always wanted to wear nice clothes. When I got dressed up with a white shirt, and a pair of new Levis, and a good-looking pair of boots, and a good hat, why I thought I was the grandest tiger in the jungle!

CHAPTER FOURTEEN

THE SIXTIES & SEVENTIES

I went to work for Earl Simpson at the WBR Ranch on the ninth day of April in 1958. I boarded in the cook-house there 'til school was out the first of June and the family could move over to join me.

That first summer there, I looked after registered cows. I rode on the cows every day, calved out a lot of them, and brought hot ones back to the bull. I didn't fool with any horses 'til the next summer when I started breaking a colt or two. Simpson was getting thirty to forty colts a year, and over the years, I worked with a lot of them. Charles, when he'd come home from school, would work with some of them too.

He'd learned how to tie up a colt's hind foot, and get in and out of the saddle, and get on him with sacks and slickers and stuff, and wool him around, and maybe drive him with a set of W's in the corral, and learn him what "whoa!" was. But, it was a square corral, and it wasn't good to ride in, so we'd take them out and drive them about five miles over the hills.

We'd go out with three horses, driving the green bronc with Charles's saddle already on. Once we'd get out there, we'd hobble Charles's horse and take the lines off the green colt, and Charles would get on him. I'd get behind on my old palomino horse, Coffee. If the colt acted like he was going to buck, I'd sail into him with a hard-twist rope to keep him galloping. If a horse is going fast, he can't drop his head and buck too good. But, most of them was pretty gentle colts and we just trotted them around, and they was used to me being right behind with the lines. We'd get them sweating out a bit, and then Charles would head him for home. I'd go back and unhobble his other horse and lead him back. After a couple of times like that, them colts would be handling so that Charles could ride them alone.

I remember one night in August, 1959, we had all gone to bed when my mother, who was staying with us, said she thought she was having a dizzy spell because she felt the bed move. Then the chickens began to squawk, and Pauline said there was something in the chicken house and I should get down there and kill it. So, I grabs the gun and goes down there, and the chicken house was all dusty, and the chickens was all on the floor, scared to death, with their wings kind of spread out, and I couldn't imagine what had happened.

A guy in the bunkhouse had just come home from town a little bit drunk, and he come out of the bunkhouse saying, "By God, there is something radical wrong 'cause my shirts is a-quivering in the clothes closet!" He thought he had the shakes.

Another guy there from California said it had been the tremor of an earthquake, and sure enough, we come to find out there had been a big one over at Yellowstone Park in Montana that shook a dam loose and killed a lot of people.

They had a two year old bull at Simpson's that had always been in a small pen or in a box stall, but they decided one day he needed more exercise, so they turned him out in a pasture where there was boggy ground with cattails in it.

Well, that bull went down into the bog and got clear up to his belly in sloppy mud. It wasn't far to solid ground, but we didn't know how to get him out of there.

First, I twisted his tail to get him to jump, but he only jumped once and kind of went in deeper. So, we put a halter on him and tied it to a jeep, figuring that if we could get him to jump again, we could pull him to solid ground. But when I twisted his tail, he wouldn't jump, and I thought maybe we'd have to get a wrecker and put a belt around him and pull him out thataway. So then, I got the "hotshot" from the barn that gives them a shock. The electricity in it isn't stout enough that it will burn them or anything, and I touched that bull under the tail, and he made a big old lunge, and we got him a little closer to solid ground before he settled back down in again. You got to be careful hotshotting animals, because if you hit them too much, they'll get mad and sull up on you. So, I let that bull lay and rest for a while, and I smoked a cigarette and fooled around, and let him get all relaxed. Then I touched him again, and he went to lunging and floundering and got his front feet on solid ground, and we got him out, the dumb son-of-a-gun.

I didn't get along very well with the foreman there. He was kind of a drinking man and not much good around livestock. He come back from town one time with a bull, and he'd stopped most of the afternoon at the Town and Country Bar. When he got back, he was drunked up, and he backed his truck up to the loading chute to unload the bull. But the chute was too high, and it was raining, and he was a big, heavy bull, and if he tried to jump the gap, he could have slipped and broke his hind legs under the chute.

"You can't do that, George," I said to the foreman.

He said, "Mr. Holmes, who is boss around this outfit?"

But, when he couldn't unload the bull that way, we took the truck down to a bank and unloaded the bull there. Then, he said he was going to saddle up a horse and take the bull out to pasture that night.

"You shouldn't do that tonight," I told him.

And he said, "Who is boss around this outfit, Mr. Holmes?"

But he didn't take the bull out that night, and next morning, I asked him when he was going to do it.

"I'm not," he said. "That's your job."

"Well last night *you* was going to take him to pasture," I told him.

"Well that was last night."

Another time, we was mothering up cows, and I had been around them enough that I could pair them up pretty quick. The foreman had this cow and calf cut out, but the cow kept wanting to run back into the bunch, and he kept keeping her back. Finally I said, "That ain't a pair, George."

He said, "Mr. Holmes, I know these cows and you ain't been here very long."

So, I bet him a fifth of whiskey, and he took the bet. The cow kept coming back, and he said, "Don't you make a damn liar out of me and make me lose that fifth!" but when she got back in the bunch, her real calf went up to her, and started sucking, and wagging his tail and all. That foreman cussed and stormed!

Then there was the time he figured a cow was still heavy wih calf and was going to take her out to pasture, but something about her told me she had calved. It can be hard to tell when they are big and fat, and they've got a tight bag that doesn't look like it's been sucked on. I told him if he took her away, he would starve her calf wherever it was. He should take her back to where she came from and let her find it. A cow will hide her calf sometimes, and it can be several days before you see it.

He said, "I suppose we'll go out there and find a calf and you'll have something more to laugh at!" And that's just how it was.

There was this Hereford cow he thought had been bred to a good yellow bull, and he wanted the calf for his show string. He told me to really watch that cow when she calved. "You better not lose that calf," he told me, "because she's going to have a bull calf, and it's going to be a good one!"

One morning I went out, and she'd had her calf . . . but it was a black baldy. An Angus bull must have got in and bred her. So I come a-riding in and I said, "You got pretty good judgment, George!"

"Has that old cow calved?" he asked.

"Yeah," I said, "and she got a bull calf."

"By God, that's good!" he said.

"But he's a little on the dark side," I said.

He couldn't believe it, and if that calf had been just a *little* dark, it wouldn't have hurt the show string too much. George had an old jeep there, and he drove to where I told him the cow and calf was at. When he saw that black calf, he came back a-cussing!

That same fall, he got to drinking too much whiskey and got himself fired.

I had to shoot a horse at Simpson's, and that was the only one I ever shot. She got hurt in the back some way, and it was awful cold, and when I come home that night, she was down and there was no way to get her up. I covered her all up with straw and blankets, and the next morning she was still alive, but I could tell she was going to die. So, I shot her to end her suffering.

I never cared for guns and killing things. I shot a deer once, because I wanted some meat, but I was never much of a hunter. Guns scare me. Charles would get a deer license and go hunting, but he never liked guns much, either. I don't know whether I'm soft hearted or what, but I just don't care about going out and shooting anything. I'd rather see animals running around.

While I was at Simpson's, I joined the Elks—probably in '59 or '60. People had wanted me to join long before that, and they was always after me to sign up, but there never was much entertainment there. By the time I joined, though, there was a place to have dinner there, and they had dancing and country music.

I always liked to dance, but I was kind of bashful for a long time and never danced much 'til I got older. It was only ten or fifteen years ago that I really got to going. During a good number of years, through the 40s and 50s when we was out to Beckton, we hardly ever went to a dance.

This was about the time our daughter, Shirley, started going to Washington, D.C. She'd been in the 4H and learned how to sew, and she made a dress for a contest called "Make It Yourself With Wool." Because of that, she went to Douglas to model the dress for the Wool Growers Association. That's where she met Keith Thompson, who was running for Congress.

Thompson asked her what she wanted to do, and Shirley said she was starting college and was going to take up secretary work. He said to call him if she ever needed help finding a job. I figured Thompson was just building votes from Shirley's old man and old lady—and he got elected, too. Then, in December of her first year at college, Shirley comes home one day and says, "Guess what! Keith Thompson wants to hire me for his secretary in Washington, D.C." Thompson liked to have bright girls that was untrained, so that he could train them the way he wanted them. And Shirley's teacher told her she should go. "You can always get a college education," she said, "but you can't always go to Washington, D.C."

So, the last day of January when Shirley was 17, she flew to Washington. Thompson spent one term as Representative, and then he run for the Senate and got elected, but he died of a heart attack before he ever took office. By then, Shirley had been in Washington two years.

During that time, she'd met a fellow called Jim Dupree, and he got her a job working for a Senator from Illinois called Finnegan. She was only with him a year when she got tired of Washington, so she quit in September of 1962, and come home, and worked in Sheridan. But, she'd been away three years, and it wasn't the same town she had left. The kids she'd known had drifted here and she had drifted there. Jim called her one night after the first of the year and told her she'd better come back and take her secretary job again with Finnegan. She did, in the middle of January sometime, and that's when she and Jim got married. She's spent the rest of her time in Washington ever since.

Shirley liked the country very much, but when she went to the city, she changed to be a city girl and didn't want to come back. She liked the bright lights. But now that she's getting older, I think she wishes her kids could grow up more in the country, and she comes out here when she can.

There's something about kids that grow up in the country—they have more endurance than city kids, because they automatically get out and do more as they get older. Country kids learn to get up early and do more things, and they build up their muscles and get stouter than the town kids.

When you are a father in the country, your kids help from the time they're little guys, even if it's only, "Go get a bucket," or "Go pick up a wrench." I always had my kids around doing little things with me, and I worked close with them. In the city, if the parents work, they just see the kids night and morning. They might go golfing, or to a ball game together, but they're not as close as they would be in the country. And country kids don't generally have other kids to play with like town kids do, so that makes the family closer, too.

I think a kid needs to learn to work early. If they just play, it can be hard when they get to be eighteen and have to work. It's hard for them to straighten out.

And country kids, from the time they can remember, learn about sex in animals and about life and death. Maybe they've got some animal they like, and it dies, and from that they learn a lot. They learn to treat animals good, too. Kids that has never been around animals don't have the faintest idea what hurts an animal. They don't know animals have any feelings. When kids get close to animals, they get more of a feeling for people. I have heard more than one guy say, that if a kid grows up with a horse and a cow, he will be a better citizen than if he don't know animals at all.

They didn't have a regular manager at Simpson's 'til I left, but it turned out they'd hired one, but never told me. Everyone started giving me the silent treatment. The herdsman there didn't like me and wanted someone else with the cows, but nobody would say anything. They just gave me the freeze out. I even asked Simpson once if he'd hired a manager, and he said no he hadn't.

Then one rainy night, the new manager pulled in with some of his registered horses, jerked my saddle horse out of his box stall, and put him out in the rain. Things hit the fan over that deal. I wasn't feeling very good anyway, so that's when I quit. It was the fall of '64.

By the time I left Simpson's, Charles was already in the Marines. The last two years of high school, he'd been wrangling dudes for Ike Fordyce at Tepee Lodge, and after he graduated, he went to Arizona for a while, wrangling dudes there. He went down the first part of November, but the dude business was poor, and after the first of the year, they had to lay somebody off, and he was the new man.

On the road back from Arizona, he got to Billings and went into the Marine recruiting office, because, if you weren't in school, you were up for the draft, and Charles had heard the Marines ran a rodeo outfit in San Diego. The next thing we knew, he had signed up for four years. For a year, he was in dry dock in San Diego, and then he went to the Gulf of Tonkin, and floated around over there for a year. He came back to the States after that and was in the Honor Guard, and they're a spit-and-polish deal. They've got to have their clothes on just right and the buttons all shined up.

One Monday night, Charles called us and said they were shipping them all to Vietnam. About midnight on Wednesday, he called again and said, "I bet you can't guess where I am at." And I said, "Well, I wouldn't know." And he said, "There's seven of us they didn't take across to Vietnam. They turned us back at the last minute, and I'm on the rodeo base out here in San Diego." So, that's where he stayed for the rest of his time, looking after the bucking horses and putting on rodeos.

That's where he met his wife Sandy. She had some job at the base. The man she was going with was sent to Vietnam and was killed shortly after. Charles used to say, "I guess he got my bullet." Anyway, Charles and Sandy were married in April of 1969.

After Simpson's, I went back to the NX for the winter. We went to visit Shirley in Washington for Christmas, but I was back by the middle of January.

At the NX, they needed someone to put out protein blocks for 400 head of heifers on a high divide off Buffalo Creek, and they was going to borrow an old sheepwagon for someone to live in up there. They couldn't get no one to take the job, so I took it. The day I went up there I took my car, and they trucked my horses up, but the sheepwagon wasn't there yet. I went out to ride and came back about three-thirty in the afternoon, and there it was with my stuff throwed inside—dishes and grub and everything—and it was twenty below zero. They'd said it was a good wagon, but you could throw a cat through the places the wind blew in.

There's not much to a sheepwagon. It has a bench inside and doors that open up where you can put canned goods. There's a little stove, and a table slides out from under the bed, and just inside the door, there is a little stand where you can set a bucket of water. The top is just canvas that's stretched over bows. I had a gas lantern and a big bedroll, and I'd throw my chaps and heavy coats back against the door, because half an inch or so was open all the way around it. It usually doesn't take much to heat a sheepwagon, but in that one I'd have to get up in the middle of the night and stoke coal into the stove. I was out there one night in a blizzard, and it snowed and blowed, and the lantern was swinging back and forth, and the wagon was moving! In the morning, I had to throw snow off the bed and there was snow all over the floor.

Being out there by myself was lonely. It was twenty miles from the main ranch and forty miles from Sheridan, and I'd come into town every Saturday after getting the water holes opened up, and get some groceries, and spend the night at home, and then go back Sunday morning about nine o'clock to open the water again.

Besides keeping the water open, my job was to block them 400 head of heifers. I'd go out in the morning with two horses loaded with blocks that weighed thirty-three and a third pounds each. You'd put six blocks on a horse in panniers, and throw them off two at a time to keep your loads balanced. In the mornings, I'd open the water holes and throw off the first load of blocks, and then get back to the wagon about eleven, and eat some chili or soup before going to scatter some more. I'd get back again about three o'clock and set on that little bed for the rest of the day. I had a radio, and that was about the size of it. In the evening, I'd make myself some steak or hamburger, and the only way to thaw out the meat was to fry it in a skillet.

Of course, there wasn't any telephone or nothing, and if a horse had fallen down with me, they wouldn't have known about it until the next week, and the crows would probably eat you up before they found you. Pauline came up and spent one night, and it was so tight for two people that one of us had to stay in bed while the other did the dishes. I was up there for two months or so, and I wouldn't want to do it again. It wasn't a very enjoyable time.

In the spring of '65, I went to work for Hoot Duncan. He'd just bought 500 or 600 yearlings, and I was supposed to look after them. They was running in an irrigated pasture, and I knew I was going to have to run the irrigation in that pasture, but when they didn't get a head irrigator that summer, I got to doing it all around there. I don't like that work. You have to be out in cold water, with rubber boots on, early in the morning and again at night. And at Duncan's, the ditches was in real bad shape, and he didn't have money or time to fix them. When you're a green irrigator like I was, there is a lot to do and it's hard work.

I never was much of a duck! I was a dry-land boy and I got scars on my feet from them damn rubber boots. They rub blisters on your feet when your socks get sweaty, and damp, and pull down inside. Regular irrigators cut up old bed blankets and kind of wrap their feet instead of buying socks, but I never tried it.

Some guys would rather irrigate than punch cows, but I'd rather be horseback where you can set up, and let your feet hang down, and kind of ride along without doing all that labor with your muscles and your back. I'd rather fence than irrigate. When you quit fencing, you don't have to worry about the fence going anywhere, but water's going to go somewhere and you have to watch it. I'd even rather calve heifers than mess around in that muddy water!

You can always tell if a guy is irrigating good, because, if he isn't, there will be places in a field that's green and other places that's dry. I had dry spots and green spots, and after the second summer, I decided it was too slow and tiresome standing out there with an irrigating shovel. So, when I heard about a job at Dick Hosford's Diamond Cross ranch at Birney, I took it. It's the only job

I ever got through an employment office, and it's a job I've had for twelve years, and probably the last one I'll ever have.

At first, I didn't do too much with the cattle on the Diamond Cross. I worked in the hayfield some, but at different times I'd get on a horse and ride here and ride there, 'til I got the country pretty well mapped up on my own. Everybody was surprised that I could get around in the hills the way I could and knew so many trails. But I grew up in a country like this, and I've been an outdoor man all my life.

There was only a small crew at the Diamond Cross then—maybe three beside myself. That first year it took the whole summer to get the branding done, and move the cattle from Four Mile over to the South Fork pastures, and we never got there 'til the first of September. Then after about a month, Dick Hosford sold them, so we had to gather them all and bring them back down again, so we could put them through the chutes and give them cold shots and get them ready for sale.

That winter it started snowing in December, and the snow got deep, and, boy, it got cold. It wasn't as bad as winters we've had since, but it hit twenty below zero one day Dick and I was out riding, and for sixteen days in January it never got above zero. I made ten trips over to South Fork to bring cattle down along the creek, and once I got them scattered in bunches, I'd drive out with a pickup and feed them hay and mineral and protein. They got pretty thin that winter, but we got by 'til March when we got a chinook wind, and the snow chinooked off and the grass came early.

That next summer, I got them all moved across to South Fork in two weeks, and since then it's been about

High summer pasture near Birney, Montana.

the same each year. You calve the cows in April, brand in June, move up to the high pastures in summer, gather the cattle in the fall, and bring them back down again—some to sell, and some to feed over the winter. So, every year it is about the same routine, around and around.

And there's always fencing. You have to check whether the gates or posts are off, and if you don't have good corner posts to stretch to, you don't have any fence. You can lose some line posts that rot off, but if you've got good corner posts, you'll still have a fence. It's a job to put in a corner post, because there can be a lot of wires

Loading Candy Spots into pickup, 1979.

on it, but you'd just as well sail into it and build a good corner, because then your fence will stand up.

I've put in so many corners on the Diamond Cross that I don't know how many it amounts to. I can ride anywhere around and see my gate and corner posts.

We were at the Diamond Cross when Charles came back from the service. For a while, he stayed out in California making good money in construction, and he said he was never going to come back on a ranch. Well, he found all he was doing on construction work was driving pickups to work and back, and helping plant trees. It got tiresome, and he got to thinking about riding horseback, so he came back to Ike Fordyce at Tepee Lodge, where he'd worked in high school.

Ray Holmes with Dick Hosford, branding, 1979.

He had some other jobs, too. He was a dispatcher on the police force for a while, and then he went to work for Northern Seed, because it paid better than the police. One winter, he worked for the highway department, and then in the spring, Jack Chase came up with a job for him running cattle at the Bar 66. He thought that was a

Ray Holmes with Diamond Cross cattle.

real good job, so he went down and worked there for three winters.

In 1973, he bought some cattle of his own, and he ran them for about a year and a half. September, 1974, was the end of his life—Friday the 13th, just after his 30th birthday.*

One of the problems over the years has been finding good help. Once this energy development got a-going, the up-and-coming boys got jobs on the mines or doing con-

*At first, Ray and Pauline were led to believe Charles had broken his neck in a fall from his horse. Later, they learned that his body had been found hanging from the branch of a tree. The coroner returned a verdict of suicide—a verdict that was met with widespread scepticism.

struction work. They make so much more money than on a ranch, and they can have Saturday and Sunday off every week. They work shorter hours, and they have time to play. A lot of these young fellows that's working at the mines are living really good. They've got boats and cabins, and they can do a lot of things in two days off. That would be a pretty nice life with every weekend off. And, when you do have to work weekends, you get paid double time.

I've never had many weekends. I can't say I didn't have some Sundays off, but I most generally had to do some kind of chores Sunday morning and night all my life. Sometimes I would go a month at a time without a day off. If you are calving, you have to work on Sunday, and if you are feeding, cows have to eat on Sunday as much as any other day. Some years, I never even had a vacation.

Some winters are a lot worse than others. The winter of 1978–1979 was really bad. We got a foot of wet snow on the ninth day of November, and it was winter all the time after that. The cattle could hardly get anything to eat from then on. It wasn't so cold up to the first of December, but then it stayed cold right on through January and a lot of February. It reached around ten or twelve below, and would never get up above zero in the daytime. And the wind blew every day.

In that bitter cold weather, cattle need an awful lot of feed to keep their bodies up just to live. We had to feed hay and supplement to them, and they still went downhill. When it stays cold all the time and there's no let-up, cattle never get a chance to warm up. The snow was so deep they couldn't get up into any protected areas. We'd throw the bales of hay off the sides of the pickup, and that would pack the snow down some, and that's where the cattle would stay—right on the feed ground. That was one of the worst winters to get around that I'd ever saw in my time, and a lot of cattle died.

It puts stress on people, too. In a winter like that, there's very little activity. You couldn't hardly get to Sheridan except with a four-wheel drive, and people don't go out very much in that sub-zero weather. After you've been out all day feeding cattle and you get in by the fire, you don't want to go back out.

Then, when you have to stay in from January to March, you start getting cabin fever. You don't see your neighbors, and it's real boring for a woman who has to set in the house all the time. Just setting in the house watching the snow falling down! It's bad enough for a man, but he gets outside at least. Of course, when you get older like me, you think about having a flat tire if you go visiting. So you don't like to go out, but it gets depressing not to talk to somebody and hear somebody else's troubles. And that's just what you hear when you do go out. The whole conversation is about the weather, or the cows getting poor, or something like that. That's what runs in your life, so you go all over the same road again and again. You'd think you'd talk about something else, but trouble is the big end of the conversation.

People in town say I should retire, and the day is coming when I will have to do that. It could be nice to be in town. Last winter, I thought how it would be to get up in the morning and figure I didn't have to do anything but set around the fire. But after a while, I'd get tired of that. Some guys could tend bar or do janitor work a few hours a day and be happy, but that wouldn't be for me.

Ray Holmes, summer 1979.

And after they're done, they go bumming around. But, I don't care to hang around a bar. That's not my life. I like to go in for a while some evening and have a few drinks, and then leave. Even the second day I go back in, the talk and the whiskey glasses get stale to me, and I don't have any fun. I'm not much of a shopper, either. I walk into a store and look around and feel kind of lost. I suppose you could adjust to a lot of that, but it would be hard.

The fellow that was running the Elks was wanting me to come in and tend bar. He said he'd soon teach me how, and that I'd make a good one, because I knew everyone and would find something funny to say to them. But after a few days of that, I'd be damn cranky. If you're not used to standing on your feet all the time, you can get plumb played out, and working a bar you'd just be walking around in small circles.

If I was financially fixed, I'd go back to the Devils Tower country where I grew up, and maybe have a place where kids could come and learn something about a ranch. It would be kind of a dude ranch. I'd have a good cookhouse and sleeping quarters, a public bathroom that would be modern, but that they'd have to walk to, and some horses and some cows. The kids would pay to come out there so you could make a go of it. They'd learn some general ranch work in the time they was there and help you keep the place up. You could teach them about fixing fence, and maybe how to put shoes on a horse. You could teach them about moving cows, how to saddle a horse, and how to hook up a team and drive them.

Father Time is already telling me to slow down, and that's what I'd like to be doing when the time comes for me to quit riding. But, I don't suppose I'll ever get to do it. I suppose me and Pauline will just move on into town like everyone else.*

*Soon after these words were recorded in 1980, Ray and Pauline did move to town. They bought a house on Clarendon Avenue in Sheridan, Wyoming. Pauline claimed she was not going to bother with a garden, but at this writing in 1992, her patio and flower garden are the envy of the neighborhood. Ray has stayed by the fire on some cold mornings, but on many others he has been out in the hills, helping old friends and neighbors to do what he and they do best—work with cattle and horses.

In November of 1991, Ray celebrated his eightieth birthday.

INDEX

All photos indicated by boldface type.